# First World War
## and Army of Occupation
# War Diary
## France, Belgium and Germany

3 INDIAN (LAHORE) DIVISION
Divisional Troops
Royal Army Medical Corps
111 Indian Field Ambulance
12 August 1914 - 31 December 1915

WO95/3920/3

The Naval & Military Press Ltd
www.nmarchive.com
Published in association with The National Archives

Published by

## The Naval & Military Press Ltd

Unit 10 Ridgewood Industrial Park,

Uckfield, East Sussex,

TN22 5QE England

Tel: +44 (0) 1825 749494

www.naval-military-press.com

www.nmarchive.com

*This diary has been reprinted in facsimile from the original. Any imperfections are inevitably reproduced and the quality may fall short of modern type and cartographic standards.*

© **Crown Copyright**
**Images reproduced by permission of The National Archives, London, England, 2015.**

# Contents

| Document type | Place/Title | Date From | Date To |
|---|---|---|---|
| Heading | WO95/3920/3 | | |
| Heading | BEF 3 Ind Lahore Div Troops No III Indian Fld Amb 1914 Aug-1915 Dec | | |
| Miscellaneous | No.III Indian Field Ambulance 1914 Aug Lahore Division Aug 1914-Dec | | |
| War Diary | Lahore Coutonbeach (Lahore) | 12/08/1914 | 12/08/1914 |
| War Diary | Lahore Cautt. | 13/08/1914 | 13/08/1914 |
| War Diary | Lahore | 14/08/1914 | 14/08/1914 |
| War Diary | Lahore Coutonbeach West | 15/08/1914 | 15/08/1914 |
| War Diary | On Train On The Way From Lahore To Karachi | 16/08/1914 | 16/08/1914 |
| War Diary | Karachi | 17/08/1914 | 28/08/1914 |
| War Diary | On Board H.M's.& H.T. Castalia | 29/08/1914 | 29/08/1914 |
| War Diary | H.M.H.T. Castalia Arabian Sea | 30/08/1914 | 08/09/1914 |
| War Diary | H.M.H.T. Castalia Red Sea | 09/09/1914 | 13/09/1914 |
| War Diary | H.M.H.T. Castalia Suez | 14/09/1914 | 15/09/1914 |
| War Diary | H.M.H.T. Castalia | 16/09/1914 | 16/09/1914 |
| War Diary | H.M.H.T. Castalia Alexandria | 17/09/1914 | 19/09/1914 |
| War Diary | Mediterranean | 20/09/1914 | 20/09/1914 |
| War Diary | H.M.H.T. Castalia Mediterranean | 21/09/1914 | 25/09/1914 |
| War Diary | Marseilles | 26/09/1914 | 26/09/1914 |
| War Diary | Camp Chateau L'Eveque A St Liouis Marseilles | 27/09/1914 | 28/09/1914 |
| War Diary | Marseilles | 29/09/1914 | 30/09/1914 |
| War Diary | Marseilles To Orleans By Train | 01/10/1914 | 03/10/1914 |
| War Diary | Orleans Camp Cercottes | 04/10/1914 | 17/10/1914 |
| War Diary | 8 p.m.& Accomplished detraining Between 8 p.m. & Midnight | 18/10/1914 | 19/10/1914 |
| War Diary | Blendecques To Wizernes | 20/10/1914 | 20/10/1914 |
| War Diary | Wizernes to Wallon Capelle | 21/10/1914 | 21/10/1914 |
| War Diary | Wallon Capelle To Bailleul | 22/10/1914 | 22/10/1914 |
| War Diary | Bailleul To Groote Vierstraat | 23/10/1914 | 23/10/1914 |
| War Diary | Groote Vierstraat | 24/10/1914 | 30/10/1914 |
| War Diary | Mille Kruis | 31/10/1914 | 31/10/1914 |
| Heading | No.III Ind. F.A. Nov 1914 | | |
| Miscellaneous | Cover For Documents. Nature Of Enclosures. | | |
| Miscellaneous | No.III Ind. F.A. Nov 1914 | | |
| War Diary | War Diary of No III Indian Field Ambulance From 1st November 1914 To 30th November 1914 Volume I | | |
| War Diary | Millekruis To Reninghelst | 01/11/1914 | 01/11/1914 |
| War Diary | Reninghelst | 02/11/1914 | 02/11/1914 |
| War Diary | Reninghelst To Strazeele | 03/11/1914 | 03/11/1914 |
| War Diary | Strazeele To Estaires | 04/11/1914 | 04/11/1914 |
| War Diary | Estaires | 05/11/1914 | 17/11/1914 |
| War Diary | Paradis | 18/11/1914 | 22/11/1914 |
| War Diary | Paradis To Essars | 23/11/1914 | 23/11/1914 |
| War Diary | Essars | 24/11/1914 | 24/11/1914 |
| War Diary | Essars To Chateau Gorre-2 Miles | 25/11/1914 | 25/11/1914 |
| War Diary | Chateau Gorre | 26/11/1914 | 30/11/1914 |
| Miscellaneous | No.III Ind F.A. Dec 1914 | | |
| Heading | Cover For Documents. Nature Of Enclosures. Medicine | | |

| | | | |
|---|---|---|---|
| Heading | War Diary of No III Indian Field Ambulance From 1-12-14 To 31-12-14 Volume Pp 37 To 48 | | |
| War Diary | Chateau Gorre | 01/12/1914 | 03/12/1914 |
| War Diary | Chateau Gorre To Hingettes | 04/12/1914 | 04/12/1914 |
| War Diary | Hingettes | 08/12/1914 | 08/12/1914 |
| War Diary | Hingette To Halte | 10/12/1914 | 16/12/1914 |
| War Diary | Halte | 16/12/1914 | 17/12/1914 |
| War Diary | Halte 1/2 Miles Horth Of Bethune On Road To Locon | 18/12/1914 | 18/12/1914 |
| War Diary | Halte | 19/12/1914 | 22/12/1914 |
| War Diary | Halte To Lozinghem | 23/12/1914 | 23/12/1914 |
| War Diary | Lozinghem | 24/12/1914 | 31/12/1914 |
| Heading | War Diary of No III. Indian Field Ambulance From 1st January 1915 To 31st January 1915 | | |
| War Diary | Lozinghem | 01/01/1915 | 30/01/1915 |
| War Diary | Lozinghem To La Miqellerie | 31/01/1915 | 31/01/1915 |
| Heading | War Diary No 111 Indian Field Ambulance From 1st February 1915 28th February 1915 | | |
| War Diary | La Miquellerie | 01/02/1915 | 28/02/1915 |
| Heading | War Diary of III Indian Field Ambulance From 1st March 1915 31st March 1915 | | |
| War Diary | La Miquellerie | 01/03/1915 | 09/03/1915 |
| War Diary | Le Cornet Malo | 10/03/1915 | 24/03/1915 |
| War Diary | Paradis | 25/03/1915 | 30/03/1915 |
| War Diary | Paradis To Zelobes | 31/03/1915 | 31/03/1915 |
| Heading | War Diary of III Indian Field Ambulance From 1st April 1915 30th April 1915 | | |
| War Diary | Zelobes | 01/04/1915 | 13/04/1915 |
| War Diary | Robecq | 14/04/1915 | 23/04/1915 |
| War Diary | Robecq To Mont Descats | 24/04/1915 | 24/04/1915 |
| War Diary | Mont Des Cats To Ouderdom | 25/04/1915 | 26/04/1915 |
| War Diary | Ouderdom To Mont Descats | 26/04/1915 | 26/04/1915 |
| War Diary | Mont Des Cats | 27/04/1915 | 30/04/1915 |
| Heading | War Diary of III Indian Field Ambulance From 1 May 1915 To 31st May 1915 | | |
| War Diary | Mont Des Cats | 01/05/1915 | 06/05/1915 |
| War Diary | Lepinette | 07/05/1915 | 21/05/1915 |
| War Diary | La Croix Marmuse | 22/05/1915 | 23/05/1915 |
| War Diary | Lepinette | 24/05/1915 | 25/05/1915 |
| War Diary | Calonne | 26/05/1915 | 31/05/1915 |
| Heading | War Diary of III Indian Field Ambulance From 1st June 1915 To 30th June 1915 | | |
| War Diary | Calonne | 01/06/1915 | 30/06/1915 |
| Heading | War Diary of III Indian Field Ambulance From 1st July 1915 To 31st July 1915 | | |
| War Diary | Calonne | 01/07/1915 | 25/07/1915 |
| War Diary | Estaires | 26/07/1915 | 31/07/1915 |
| Heading | War Diary of III Indian Field Ambulance From 1st August 1915 To 31st August 1915 | | |
| War Diary | Estaires | 01/08/1915 | 02/08/1915 |
| War Diary | Zelobes | 03/08/1915 | 31/08/1915 |
| Heading | War Diary of III Indian Field Ambulance From 1st September 1915 To 30th September 1915 | | |
| War Diary | Zelobes | 01/09/1915 | 30/09/1915 |
| Miscellaneous | Appendix I | 24/09/1915 | 24/09/1915 |
| Miscellaneous | Appendix II | 30/09/1915 | 30/09/1915 |

| | | | |
|---|---|---|---|
| Heading | War Diary of III Indian Field Ambulance From 1st October 1915 To 31st October 1915 | | |
| War Diary | Zelobes | 01/10/1915 | 04/10/1915 |
| War Diary | Lagorgue | 04/10/1915 | 19/10/1915 |
| War Diary | Caudescure | 19/10/1915 | 31/10/1915 |
| Heading | War Diary of III Indian Field Ambulance From 1st November 1915 To 30th November 1915 | | |
| War Diary | Caudescure | 01/11/1915 | 08/11/1915 |
| War Diary | Fontes | 09/11/1915 | 20/11/1915 |
| War Diary | Les.Tourbiers | 21/11/1915 | 28/11/1915 |
| War Diary | Enquin | 29/11/1915 | 29/11/1915 |
| War Diary | Boncourt | 30/11/1915 | 30/11/1915 |
| Heading | War Diary of III Indian Field Ambulance From 1/12/15 To 31/12/15 (Volume) | | |
| War Diary | Boncourt | 01/12/1915 | 12/12/1915 |
| War Diary | Marseilles | 13/12/1915 | 14/12/1915 |
| War Diary | At Sea | 15/12/1915 | 27/12/1915 |
| War Diary | Suez | 27/12/1915 | 31/12/1915 |

130 85 / 84 OC / 3420 / 3

BEF

3 IND LAHORE DIV TROOPS

No 111 INDIAN FLD AMB

1914 AUG — 1915. DEC

To MESOPOTAMIA

No. 111. Indian Field Ambulance

1914 AUG
Lahore Division

Aug 15th – Oct

Army Form C. 2118.

Confidential

# WAR DIARY
## or
## INTELLIGENCE SUMMARY. ?.M.S.

Comdg. No 7 M.S. Section of Field Ambulance
(Erase heading not required.)

Instructions regarding War Diaries and Intelligence Summaries are contained in F. S. Regs., Part II, and the Staff Manual respectively. Title pages will be prepared in manuscript.

From the Summary of Events and Information, 1914 to

| Hour, Date, Place. | | Remarks and references to Appendices. |
|---|---|---|
| 8 A.M. 12.8.14. Saharanpur (LAHORE) | Arrived at Lahore Cantonment and reported to the A.D.M.S. 3rd (Lahore) Divisional Infantry. Was to proceed with the Mobilization of N.7 M.S. Field Ambulance commencing at 7 A.M. tomorrow as the Indian Mobilization Scheme. Weather unusually cool for this date — fine — Cool. | A.D.M.S. Lt.Col. J.W.G.A. [signature] |
| Lahore Cantt. 13.8.14. 7 A.M. to 8 P.M. | Busy all day mobilizing No.7 M.S. F.A. Personnel gradually arriving — Lieut. J.S. ANDERSON, I.M.S. returned to duty from early evening. Weather fine but rainy evg. | [signature] |
| LAHORE 14.8.14. 7 A.M. to 8.30 P.M. | Completed mobilization of No.7 M.S. F.A. and moved it at 8 P.M. from Medical Mob. depot to Stores to river at 2nd Punjabis in place of last vaccination 7.30 P.M. by the A.D.M.S. 3rd Iron Division — Weather much hotter — | [signature] |

Gulab Singh & Sons, Calcutta—No. 22 Army C.—5-8-14—1,07,000.

**Army Form C. 2118.**

# WAR DIARY
## — or —
## INTELLIGENCE SUMMARY.
*(Erase heading not required.)*

Instructions regarding War Diaries and Intelligence Summaries are contained in F. S. Regs., Part II, and the Staff Manual respectively. Title pages will be prepared in manuscript.

| Hour, Date, Place. | Summary of Events and Information. | Remarks and references to Appendices. |
|---|---|---|
| LAHORE (Cantonment West)<br>9.30 a.m. 15.8.14. | Entrained No 111 Indian Field Ambulance.—<br>Capt. C. H. Reinhold, I.M.S., and Lieut. R. M. PORTER<br>(REINHOLD)<br>I.M.S., joined for duty.— | |
| 15.8.1914 —<br>10.30 a.m. | Started for Karachi.— (KARACHI) | |
| 10.30 a.m. to 12 midnight | On the way to Karachi by train — No 94 & 8 British Field Ambulances and No 112 & 113 Indian Field Ambulances were on the same train with No 111.<br>9.9.a. — Weather very hot — No arrangements were made for food & drink at halting places, no ice and no mineral waters were available on the train — Much inconvenience resulted.— No information G.M.F. — Could be obtained today from Board of train as to where train will make stops for meals tomorrow — G.M.F. — | |

Army Form C. 2118.

# WAR DIARY
## or
## INTELLIGENCE SUMMARY.

*(Erase heading not required.)*

Instructions regarding War Diaries and Intelligence Summaries are contained in F. S. Regs., Part II, and the Staff Manual respectively. Title pages will be prepared in manuscript.

| Hour, Date, Place. | Summary of Events and Information. | Remarks and references to Appendices. |
|---|---|---|
| On train on the way from LAHORE to KARACHI. 16.8.1914 midnight to midnight | As yesterday — no arrangements were made for food and drink at halting places; no ice and no mineral waters were available on the train. Weather exceedingly hot while passing through the SIND desert. — CMM | |
| Karachi. (KARACHI) 17.8.1914 | Arrived at 9 a.m. and went into the Rest Camp. — Capt. W. H. ODLUM, I.M.S., joined. Weather cool, fresh breeze from the sea; Camp duty. — CMM | |

Army Form C. 2118.

# WAR DIARY
## INTELLIGENCE SUMMARY.
*(Erase heading not required.)*

| Hour, Date, Place. | Summary of Events and Information. | Remarks and references to Appendices. |
|---|---|---|
| KARACHI 18.8.1914 to 28.8.1914. | In rest-Camp - Excellent water supply, good allotment of tents, sound Sanitary arrangements - Very dusty in Camp; this cannot be avoided. (PORTER) Lieut. R.R.M. Porter, I.M.S., was placed on the sick list, suffering from diarrhoea, on the 20.8.14, and was transferred to the Station Hospital - He recovered and returned to duty on the 24.8.14; but on the 27.8.14 Lieut. A. KENNEDY, I.M.S., relieving Lieut. Porter, and took up duty with this Field Ambulance - Very cool fresh breeze from the sea day and night - thick clouds occasionally. | |

Army Form C. 2118.

# WAR DIARY
## INTELLIGENCE SUMMARY.
(Erase heading not required.)

Instructions regarding War Diaries and Intelligence Summaries are contained in F. S. Regs., Part II, and the Staff Manual respectively. Title pages will be prepared in manuscript.

5

| Hour, Date, Place. | Summary of Events and Information. | Remarks and references to Appendices. |
|---|---|---|
| KARACHI. 18.8.1914 to 28.8.1914. | but no rain. All ranks very healthy. No sickness at all. I was ordered to be ready to entrain at short notice any time after 12 noon on the 27.8.14, at 2.30 p.m. I was informed that my Field Ambulance would not entrain (for the port of embarkation) until next day the 28.8.14. Accordingly in the morning - On the 28.8.14 all the personnel of the Field Ambulance was helped to be in readiness from 8 a.m., an Officer of the 8 British Field Ambulance being required to be at the port of embarkation, Keamari docks (KEAMARI) at that time - Eventually No 111 B.F.A. (with No 7 + 8 British and No 112 & 113 F.A. (remaining) & No 113 Indian Field Ambulances entrained at the Pich Camp at 10.30, started at 2.30. [signature] | |

Gulab Singh & Sons, Calcutta—No. 22 Army C.—5-8-14—1,07,000.

# WAR DIARY

## INTELLIGENCE SUMMARY.

*(Erase heading not required.)*

Army Form C. 2118.

| Hour, Date, Place. | Summary of Events and Information. | Remarks and references to Appendices. |
|---|---|---|
| KARACHI 18.8.14 to 28.8.1914 | Arrived at KEAMARI docks at 3.15 p.m. were not allowed to lift the men [off?] of the train until 5 p.m., did not begin to put their material on board until 7.30 p.m., had to put most of the material on board until after dark, and all the men were not on board until after midnight, had the Indians got their evening meal and none of them had a comfortable meal in the morning as they had been in readiness at & after 8 a.m. This was a bad day for them, and much inconvenience would have been saved if the Embarkation Staff could have made a fair approximate estimate of the date and hour of embarking. Embarked on board H. M. S. Hired Transport CASTALIA (ANCHOR LINE) [signature] | 6 |

Army Form C. 2118.

# WAR DIARY
or
## INTELLIGENCE SUMMARY.
(Erase heading not required.)

Instructions regarding War Diaries and Intelligence Summaries are contained in F. S. Regs., Part II, and the Staff Manual respectively. Title pages will be prepared in manuscript.

| Hour, Date, Place. | Summary of Events and Information. | Remarks and references to Appendices. |
|---|---|---|
| On Board H.M.'s H.T. CASTALIA. 29.8.1914. | Cast off moorings at 1.30 p.m. and put to sea with six other Troop Transports, escorted by H.M.S. NORTHBROOK. — Weather cool — / great breeze from the S.W. — moderate sea — most of the Indians on board desperately sea-sick — SMM | |
| H.M.H.T. CASTALIA. 30.8.1914. ARABIAN SEA. | Covered 157 knots to noon today — weather — seasons Indian ranks broken still with sea-sickness — a question arose as to whether Indian Sub-Assistant Surgeons, who rank as warrant officers of the Indian Army, should be given Cabin accommodation before British sergeants (N.C. Os). and undecided by the officers of the S.A. Surgeons — there was not sufficient Cabin accommodation for both S.A. Surgeons British sergeants — SMM | |

Army Form C. 2118.

# WAR DIARY
or
## INTELLIGENCE SUMMARY.
(Erase heading not required.)

Instructions regarding War Diaries and Intelligence Summaries are contained in F. S. Regs., Part II, and the Staff Manual respectively. Title pages will be prepared in manuscript.

| Hour, Date, Place. | Summary of Events and Information. | Remarks and references to Appendices. |
|---|---|---|
| H.M.H.T. CASTALIA. 31.8.1914. ARABIAN Sea | All personnel drilled & exercised in progressive drill between 8 a.m. & 10 a.m. — Indians gradually recovering from sea-sickness — O.C. Troops falls round the ship at 10.15 a.m. daily; all men are cleanly out of hulas, and all bedding &c rolled up and put away tidily before his inspection. This continues is an excellent plan — Anything and fighting/matches between decks &c in the holders are strictly prohibited. Weather pleasantly cool, no rain, fresh breeze from S.W. An overhead. Covered 173 Knots to noon today — | GMc— |
| 1.9.1914. | Saw a shark cruising round the ship this morning — Classes of Officers of the R.A.M.C. and of the R.M.S. are held daily at 11 a.m. for the purpose of going through R.A.M.C. Training & Field Service Regulations &c. Covered 181 Knots to noon today — | GMc— |

Army Form C. 2118.

# WAR DIARY
## or
## INTELLIGENCE SUMMARY.
*(Erase heading not required.)*

Instructions regarding War Diaries and Intelligence Summaries are contained in F. S. Regs., Part II, and the Staff Manual respectively. Title pages will be prepared in manuscript.

| Hour, Date, Place. | Summary of Events and Information. | Remarks and references to Appendices. |
|---|---|---|
| H.M.H.T. CASTALIA 2.9.1914. ARABIAN Sea | Run to noon: 168 Knots – Quite coldish, temperature in dining saloon at 4 p.m. 75°. Drills, classes &c as usual – | |
| 3.9.1914. | Run: 162 Knots – Major Gibson R.A.M.C. was transferred today at 10:30 a.m. to H.M.H.T. Dongola to operate upon a man suffering from strangulated hernia – Operation successful – Instructed all personnel of No.III. I.B.F.A in the method of putting on a Life Belt. | |
| 4.9.1914 – | Run: 181 Knots – All S.A. Surgeons are receiving instruction daily in the work of a Field Ambulance in War – Weather somewhat hotter, temperature 80° in dining saloon at 4 p.m. | |

Army Form C. 2118.

# WAR DIARY
## INTELLIGENCE SUMMARY.
*(Erase heading not required.)*

Instructions regarding War Diaries and Intelligence Summaries are contained in F.S. Regs., Part II, and the Staff Manual respectively. Title pages will be prepared in manuscript.

| Hour, Date, Place. | Summary of Events and Information. | Remarks and references to Appendices. |
|---|---|---|
| H.M.H.T. CASTALIA 5.9.1914. ARABIAN Sea | Run: 212 Knots - Usual routine of work + instruction. Weather - 87° in dining saloon at 4 p.m. Convoy joined by H.M.S. Chatham this evening | |
| 6.9.1914 - | Run: 207 Knots - Divine Service at 11 a.m. Arrived ADEN at 3 p.m. - We have now learned for the first time that we are bound for MARSEILLES - Mess Ship is so crowded that the only place available as a Hospital is the Smoking Room on the Promenade deck. This has proved sufficient for requirements so far. | |
| 7.9.1914 - | Left ADEN at 8 p.m. - Some doubt existed up to that time as to whether the Sear work 20ft & clear for us. Very hot. | |
| 8.9.1914 | Passed PERIM at 8 a.m. Run to noon: 136 Knots - Head wind today & heat tolerable - Temperature in dining Saloon 90° | |

Army Form C. 2118.

# WAR DIARY
## INTELLIGENCE SUMMARY.
*(Erase heading not required.)*

Instructions regarding **War** Diaries and Intelligence Summaries are contained in F. S. Regs., Part II, and the Staff Manual respectively. Title pages will be prepared in manuscript.

| Hour, Date, Place. | Summary of Events and Information. | Remarks and references to Appendices. |
|---|---|---|
| H.M.H.T. CASTALIA. RED SEA. 9.9.1914. | Run to noon; 229 Knots. Head wind and heat tolerable. Temperature in Saloon; 9/0. The prophylactic administration of quinine to all ranks will commence tomorrow — dose 5 grs. daily to every man. Usual routine. Drills & exercises at 8a.m. Inspection of ship by O.C. Troops at 10:15am. Throughout the day classes of instruction in French, in R.A.M.C. Training, F.S. Regs Pts I & II. and Indian Supplement — instruction of all ranks in the application of the first field dressing, and of a selected class in first aid to wounded. Sanitation &c. Soldiers Pay Books are being prepared. EMN | /1 |

Army Form C. 2118.

# WAR DIARY
## or
## INTELLIGENCE SUMMARY.

(Erase heading not required.)

Instructions regarding War Diaries and Intelligence Summaries are contained in F. S. Regs., Part II, and the Staff Manual respectively. Title pages will be prepared in manuscript.

| Hour, Date, Place. | Summary of Events and Information. | Remarks and references to Appendices. |
|---|---|---|
| H.M.H.T. CASTALIA. RED SEA. 10.9.1914. | Run to noon; 217 Knots. Head wind – Getting Cooler – Temperature in Saloon; 88°. Usual routine – | EMM |
| 11.9.1914. | Run to noon; 202 Knots. Head wind – Getting Cooler. Temperature in Saloon; 86°. Last evening, about 8 o'clock, passed opposite Mecca. Mahommedans were informed and were allowed to come up on the Promenade deck to pray, facing east, towards Mecca. They all appreciated this very much, and are most grateful to Lt. Colonel E. Coffin R.S. for his kindness in thinking of it. The Captain of the Ship, Captain Mitchell, was found dead in his bed this morning, the temperature of his body being 103° when it was found. It is thought that he died of heat-stroke; he had been ailing for some days. He was buried at Sea at 10 a.m. EMM |  |

**Army Form C. 2118.**

# WAR DIARY
## INTELLIGENCE SUMMARY.
*(Erase heading not required.)*

Instructions regarding War Diaries and Intelligence Summaries are contained in F. S. Regs., Part II, and the Staff Manual respectively. Title pages will be prepared in manuscript.

/3

| Hour, Date, Place. | Summary of Events and Information. | Remarks and references to Appendices. |
|---|---|---|
| H.M.H.T. CASTALIA RED SEA 12.9.1914. | Run to noon: 222 Knots. Head wind. (Colr. 86°). at about 6.30 p.m. a suspicious looking vessel approached us — when she came near us suddenly whabout and fled. The Chatham (H.M.S.) on once pursued her. No information as to what happened. H.M.S. CHATHAM has returned. | BMM |
| 13.9.1914. | Run to noon: 218 Knots. Head wind — Cooler, 82° in Saloon — I have never before known the Red Sea so kind in temperature, with a head wind all the way from PERIM it has never been so cool. During terrific events at 11 a.m. saw a whale spouting at 5 p.m. in the Gulf of Suez. Inspected all ranks for inoculation against small-pox today. Arrived Suez about 8.30 p.m. In consequence of a rumour that mines were laid in the Canal we steered an unusual course, keeping close to Western shore, in single file instead of two lines. | BMM |

Gulab Singh & Sons, Calcutta—No. 22 Army C.—5-8-14—1,07,000.

Army Form C. 2118.

# WAR DIARY
— of —
## INTELLIGENCE SUMMARY.

*(Erase heading not required.)*

Instructions regarding War Diaries and Intelligence Summaries are contained in F. S. Regs., Part II, and the Staff Manual respectively. Title pages will be prepared in manuscript.

| Hour, Date, Place. | Summary of Events and Information. | Remarks and references to Appendices. |
|---|---|---|
| H.M.H.T. CASTALIA SUEZ 14.9.14 | At SUEZ all day – Fine, warm – All fighting troops are disembarking to proceed by rail to CAIRO, including the 3rd Ind. Divl. Signalling Coy. from this ship – Remainder on board CASTALIA C.114 Field ambulances, British & Indian, 9th Mule Corps &c) are to proceed by sea (via Suez Canal) to ALEXANDRIA. | |
| 15. 9. 14 – | Left SUEZ at 8 a.m. arrived PORT SAID 8 p.m. H.M.S. CHATHAM caught up the ship that the chased in the RED SEA on the 12th inst. and found her to be a harmless bound British Steamer. Mistook us for foreigners in the twilight & Bed-noticed, while coming through the Suez Canal today that it is guarded by patrols of the 19th Punjabis Rifles in the Southern half and by the 3rd Dragoon Guards in the Northern – | |

Army Form C. 2118.

# WAR DIARY
## or
## INTELLIGENCE SUMMARY.

(Erase heading not required.)

| Hour, Date, Place. | Summary of Events and Information. | Remarks and references to Appendices. |
|---|---|---|
| H.M.H.T. CASTALIA 16.9.1914 | PORT SAID to ALEXANDRIA - 6 a.m. to 9 p.m. - Fine, cool - Temperature 73°. In writing about the embarkation at KARACHI on the 2.8.14, I am not sure that I made the following point quite clear. At first every British Sergeant went first into Cabins, later a claim was made on behalf of Indian Sub-Assistant-Surgeons, urging that they, as Warrant Officers on the Indian Army, should have precedence of British N.C.Os for Cabin accommodation. This claim was upheld. The British Sergeants were ensted and the Indian Sub-Assistant Surgeons installed in their Cabins. It would be well if a fixed & published rule in charge obviated the recurrence of an incident like this - EMcM | 15 |

# WAR DIARY
## INTELLIGENCE SUMMARY.
*(Erase heading not required.)*

Army Form C. 2118.

| Hour, Date, Place. | Summary of Events and Information. | Remarks and references to Appendices. |
|---|---|---|
| H.M.H.T. CASTALIA 17.9.1914. ALEXANDRIA | Entered docks and tied up alongside wharf - animals (mules & horses) being fairly well and army Rovers (men instructed) practicing in stretcher drill - | |
| 18.9.14. | As above - weather fine and pleasantly cool - | |
| 19.9.14. | Sailed today from Alexandria for MARSEILLES. 16 transports under care of H.M.S. WEYMOUTH - Fine, calm, pleasantly warm - | |
| 20.9.14. MEDITERRANEAN | Fine, calm, pleasantly warm - our convoy was joined last evening by H.M.S. Indomitable with six transports - We hear that four Turkish warships, including the GOEBEN & BRESLAU, lately German, have come out through the DARDENELLES, and that TURKEY is about to join the GERMANS & AUSTRIANS in the war - | Run to noon: 198 knots - |

Army Form C. 2118.

# WAR DIARY
# or
# INTELLIGENCE SUMMARY.

(Erase heading not required.)

17

| Hour, Date, Place. | Summary of Events and Information. | Remarks and references to Appendices. |
|---|---|---|
| H.M.H.T. CASTALIA MEDITERRANEAN 21.9.1914 | Fine, Calm, pleasantly warm - H.M.S. INDOMITABLE left this convoy last night for the DARDENELLES. Run to noon: 218 Knots - | H.M.S. INDOMITABLE DARDENELLES. |
| 22.9.1914. | Run to noon: 215 Knots - We have been altering our course slightly at frequent intervals during the last 24 hours - At 4 p.m. we met a convoy of 13 ships from home, carrying Territorial Troops to Egypt, escorted by H.M.S. MINERVA, which turned about and is now escorting us to Egypt. H.M.S. WEYMOUTH is going back to Egypt. It was a fine sight to see in mid-ocean the 43 transports from home meeting the 25 transports from India with the two escorting warships - Fine, Calm, pleasant temperature. | |
| 23.9.1914. | Run to noon: 188 Knots - At 12 noon passed Valetta Malta - H.M.S. MINERVA went into harbour here and we proceeded without escort. I saw some warships in VALETTA harbour - one at least was flying the French flag - | VALETTA |

Army Form C. 2118.

# WAR DIARY
## INTELLIGENCE SUMMARY.
(Erase heading not required.)

Instructions regarding War Diaries and Intelligence Summaries are contained in F. S. Regs., Part II, and the Staff Manual respectively. Title pages will be prepared in manuscript.

| Hour, Date, Place. | Summary of Events and Information. | Remarks and references to Appendices. |
|---|---|---|
| H.M.H.T. Castalia. Mediterranean. 24.9.1914. | Run to noon: 220 Knots – Fine, coldish, head-breeze – Our escort H.M.S. MINERVA reported us at 8 A.M. yesterday – One case of pneumonia has developed today among the Indians of my unit, and in one case a diphtheritic sore has developed; otherwise there has been no sickness of a serious character since we left KARACHI on the 29th August – | [initials] |
| 25.9.1914 | Run to noon: 232 Knots – Fine, calm, coldish – | [initials] |
| 26.9.1914 MARSEILLES | Arrived at Marseilles this morning and was ordered to take my field ambulance at once to CHATEAU L'EVEQUE à Saint Louis in Marseilles, to evacuate there, open up immediately and receive all the sick Indians of the whole of the 3rd (Lahore) Division – This was rendered necessary by the fact that no R.A.M.C. or base hospital has yet arrived here – Pitched Camp in evening – Received sick: 16 fighting men + 15 followers – | [initials] |

Gulab Singh & Sons, Calcutta—No. 22 Army C.—5-8-14—1,07,000.

Army Form C. 2118.

19

# WAR DIARY
## or
## INTELLIGENCE SUMMARY.
*(Erase heading not required.)*

Instructions regarding War Diaries and Intelligence Summaries are contained in F. S. Regs., Part II, and the Staff Manual respectively. Title pages will be prepared in manuscript.

| Hour, Date, Place. | Summary of Events and Information. | Remarks and references to Appendices. |
|---|---|---|
| Camp CHATEAU MAGEVEQUE à St LOUIS, MARSEILLES 27.9.14. | I am receiving here my full ambulance all the Indian sick (fighting men and followers) of the Lahore Division. It is an advantage to keep a hospital. There is a good slope in the ground, and drainage ought to be satisfactory. No. Y British Field Ambulance is careful always to me, receiving British sick from the Lahore Division. The two field ambulances are the only units in camp here. Sick: fighting men 19. Followers 22. Weather fine and warm by day. Clear & cold by night, with heavy dew — | [signature] |
| 28.9.14. | Sick: fighting men 22. followers 24. Weather fine & warm. Several cases (a dozen) of Pneumonia including two men who arrived by boat — | [signature] |

Army Form C. 2118.

# WAR DIARY
## INTELLIGENCE SUMMARY.
*(Erase heading not required.)*

Instructions regarding War Diaries and Intelligence Summaries are contained in F. S. Regs., Part II, and the Staff Manual respectively. Title pages will be prepared in manuscript.

| Hour, Date, Place. | Summary of Events and Information. | Remarks and references to Appendices. |
|---|---|---|
| MARSEILLES, 29.9.1914. | Same camp at Chateau l'Evêque – Strong wind from N.W. during last night and all day today – No rain, some clouds – Sek: fighting may followers 32 – | 41 |
| 30.9.1914 – Marseilles – | Same Camp at Chateau l'Evêque – Fine and warm by day, clear & cold at night – No 128 I.F.A. arrived in this Camp at 6.30 P.M. and took over sick and a quantity of rifles and ammunition from me – No 111 I.F. Ambulance is under orders to entrain tomorrow morning at 10 A.M. at the Gare D'ARENC and proceed Northwards – I am leaving behind at MARSEILLES eight sick men of my own unit, Viz. 1 Hindu and seven Army Bearers – They are in No 128 Indian Casualties up to date – Lt Col: I.M.S. Comdg No 111 I.F.A. | |

Gulab Singh & Sons, Calcutta—No. 22 Army C—5-8-14—1,07,000

Army Form C. 2118.

# WAR DIARY

## INTELLIGENCE SUMMARY.

(Erase heading not *required*.)

No. 111 Ind. Field Ambulance.

**Confidential** — 21

Instructions regarding War Diaries and Intelligence Summaries are contained in F. S. Regs., Part II, and the Staff Manual respectively. Title pages will be prepared in manuscript.

| Hour, Date, Place. | Summary of Events and Information. | Remarks and references to Appendices. |
|---|---|---|
| MARSEILLES to ORLEANS by train — 1.10.1914 to 3.10.1914. | Struck camp at the Château D'If gorge early in the morning on the 1st Oct. Entrained at the GARE D'ARENE at 10.15 a.m., started at 2.25 p.m. The only scheduled half of the train on the 1st was at CETTE from 9.56 p.m. to 10.41 p.m. There were then occasional short halts, but when at fixed for all purposes. Cooked rations for the day were carried by the men. On the 2nd Oct. halts were made at NARBONNE 1.31 a.m. to 2.45 a.m., BRAM 6.35 a.m. to 7.45 a.m., TOULOUSE 10.25 p.m. to 12 p.m. (when all men cooked their food (for the day) & MONTAUBAN 3.51 p.m. to 3.21 p.m. There were no other scheduled halts, but occasional short halts were made which sufficed for every purpose. On the 3rd October halts were made at ST SULPICE LAURIÈRE 5.45 a.m. to 7.53 a.m. & ARGENTON 10.23 a.m. to 1.31 p.m. (when all men cooked their food for the whole day) — There were no other scheduled halts on the 3rd but occasional short halts were made which were sufficient for all purposes — The train arrived at LES AUBRAIS station ORLEANS at 7.27 p.m., and marched out to camp at CERCOTTES their huts. But where we got settled down by 11 p.m. The arrangements along the railway | |

Army Form C. 2118.

22

# WAR DIARY
## or
## INTELLIGENCE SUMMARY.

(Erase heading not required.)

Instructions regarding War Diaries and Intelligence Summaries are contained in F. S. Regs., Part II, and the Staff Manual respectively. Title pages will be prepared in manuscript.

| Hour, Date, Place. | Summary of Events and Information. | Remarks and references to Appendices. |
|---|---|---|
| 1.10.1914 to 3.10.1914. | Line for cooking food, both for Indians & Europeans, for watering men and horses, and for washing were excellent. Twice the ammunition officer of the train which carried Revier No. 111 9.2. Ambulance, No. 7 British field Ambulance commanded by Lt. Col. L. MAY, R.A.M.C., and a Veterinary hospital commanded by Capt. STEELE A.V.C. a British Guard under a Sergeant was posted in a brake van immediately behind the engine and an Indian guard under a havildar in a brake van at the rear of the train. The stretcher doolie was manhandled and nobody was allowed to get off the train without my permission. Weather delightful, functioning— |
| 4.10.14 – ORLEANS. Camp CERCOTTES | In camp with the Colors Piroux, myself Lut. Young and tea sick of Indians. Lt. Pte. 119.9.F.O. is doing the duty here for the Indian ack of the 1st division as I did so at Marseilles. Sly orders Ambulance trains, Collecting & Carrying wounded to | |

Gulab Singh & Sons, Calcutta—No. 22 Army C.—5-8-14—1,07,000.

Army Form C. 2118.

23

# WAR DIARY
or
## INTELLIGENCE SUMMARY.
*(Erase heading not required.)*

Instructions regarding War Diaries and Intelligence Summaries are contained in F. S. Regs., Part II, and the Staff Manual respectively. Title pages will be prepared in manuscript.

| Hour, Date, Place. | Summary of Events and Information. | Remarks and references to Appendices. |
|---|---|---|
| Camp CERCOTTES, ORLEANS. 5.10.14. | As on 4.10.14. Also equipping, & fitting members to. Weather very fine; no rain; freezes every night. | CMM |
| 9.10.14. | Daily routine as on 4 & 5.10.14. Prince Arthur of Connaught rode through the camps of the Division today. Froze very hard last night. | CMM |
| 11.10.14 to 12.10.14 | Daily routine every day as on 4, 5, 10.14 eh is most useful to have an opportunity of training Army Bearers in working with stretchers & ambulance wagons. Searching for wounded, applying its field dressing &c. All the warm clothing authorised for Indians is not yet available but is gradually being acquired. | CMM |
| 13.10.14. | 9 F.A. my field Ambulance out today (8 a.m. to 7 p.m.) with the 8th (Jullundur) Infantry Brigade, commanded by Major General P.M. Carnegy, C.B. - Practised the collection and evacuation of wounded from the battlefield to the Rear our Division nr the field Ambulance. Some rain last night & today. | CMM |

Gulab Singh & Sons, Calcutta—No. 22 Army C.—5-8-14—1,07,000.

Army Form C. 2118.

# WAR DIARY
## INTELLIGENCE SUMMARY.
(Erase heading not required.)

Instructions regarding War Diaries and Intelligence Summaries are contained in F.S. Regs., Part II, and the Staff Manual respectively. Title pages will be prepared in manuscript.

24.

| Hour, Date, Place. | Summary of Events and Information. | Remarks and references to Appendices. |
|---|---|---|
| Camp CERCOTTES, Orleans 14.10.14 to 16.10.14. | Some rain during the night 13-14; heavy rain afternoon 14th. The wind backed to the South-west on 13th. Until the 13th it froze every night. It is less cold now by night. — Usual routine of 6 & 8 a.m. drug & gymnastic and boots, clothing, blankets &c., and with training & inspecting Army Reserves in the work of carrying & loading in wagons the stretchers &c. which they now have for this campaign, and which they are quite unaccustomed to — Much time is most useful for these purposes. — JMP | |
| 17.10.14 | Busy selecting surplus baggage & stores & here; packing of remainder; loading up wagons to entrain tonight. — Marched our of camp in rain, just darkness at 6 p.m. to entrain at Orleans — our central station, entrained with loaded wagons 10 p.m. to 1 a.m. — Started at 1 a.m. by train for the north. — JMP | |
| 18 & 19.10.14 — x 8 A.M. accomplished detraining between 8 A.M. & midnight — JMP | By train from Orleans to BLENDECQUES near St OMER — via ⊕ PARIS, Rouen, Abbeville, Boulogne, Calais & St Omer. Arrived at BLendecques at afternoon — accommodation for train not good — 5 officers were provided by car down — accommodation for carts & such were confined for 4 hours by a railway carriage accident of a platform which was extremely injury. — JMP | |

Army Form C. 2118.

# WAR DIARY
or
INTELLIGENCE SUMMARY.

(Erase heading not required.)

Instructions regarding War Diaries and Intelligence Summaries are contained in F. S. Regs., Part II, and the Staff Manual respectively. Title pages will be prepared in manuscript.

25

| Hour, Date, Place. | Summary of Events and Information. | Remarks and references to Appendices. |
|---|---|---|
| 20.10.14 BLENDECQUES to WIZERNES | 4 Kilometres – went into billets at Wizernes and took in all Indian dick of the Division – Driver Harding A.S. Corps, missed the train and was left behind at Calais yesterday – A baggage wagon slipped off the ramp and had a wheel broken (in detraining last night in the dark on an open railway line (no living platform) at Blendecques – I placed the wagon at once in the hands of a Wheelwright (Winbrough, Frederic Duprot) at Blendecques to have a new wheel made, informing the R.T.O. at Blendecques of the matter – | |
| 21.10.14 WIZERNES to WALLON CAPELLE | Despatched 23 Indian sick to railway station at Wizernes at 2 A.M. for transfer to some hospital unknown to me – Marched at 2.30 A.M. and arrived and billeted up in the wilds at 1 A.M. close to the headquarters of the 7th Infantry Brigade – No billets were allotted. | |

Army Form C. 2118.

# WAR DIARY

War Diary of No.

## INTELLIGENCE SUMMARY.

Lt. Col. Shore, A.M.S.
Confd. N.W. 9. 2.9.
(Erase heading not required.)

26.
Confidential.

from 22.10.14

Instructions regarding War Diaries and Intelligence Summaries are contained in F. S. Regs., Part II, and the Staff Manual respectively. Title pages will be prepared in manuscript.

| Hour, Date, Place. | Summary of Events and Information. | Remarks and references to Appendices. |
|---|---|---|
| 22.10.14 – WAR DIV CAPELLE to BAILLEUL – | Marched at 7 A.M. – to HAZEBROUCK and arrived at billets in BAILLEUL at 5 P.M. Fine weather | Lieut. Smith EF & 21 F.M.S. Conf. N.W. 9. |
| 23.10.14 – BAILLEUL to GROOTE VIERSTRAAT – | Marched at 6 A.M. – to NEWE EGLISE – KEMMEL – Crossed Belgian border at 10 A.M. Arrived at GROOTE VIERSTRAAT at 1 P.M. – Billeted in farm & opened tent division. Sub-divisions in afternoon sent to WYTSCHAETE and to HOLLEBEKE – went to latter place myself – 11 wounded and 2 sick were brought into my field ambulance before midnight – Attention! I am attached to the 7th Infy. Bde and have with me one tent sub-division and the whole of the Bearer Division. The front tent sub-division is with the headquarters of the Cavalry Division which has gone in a different direction from us – EMR | |
| 24.10.14 – GROOTE VIERSTRAAT | Despatched 15 wounded & 4 sick at 1 P.M. to Clearing Hospital at HAZEBROUCK. Admitted today 9 wounded + 5 sick – went out at 9 A.M. under instructions of a general action was believed to be imminent – Having visited the trenches of the 12th & 14th Bdes this at Hollebeke yesterday evening I went to see the trenches of the 5th Rifles at Wytschaete this evening for the purpose of learning the lie | |

Gulab Singh & Sons, Calcutta—No. 22 Army C.—5-8-14—L 07-000

# WAR DIARY or INTELLIGENCE SUMMARY.

Army Form C. 2118.

27.

| Hour, Date, Place. | Summary of Events and Information. | Remarks and references to Appendices. |
|---|---|---|
| 24.10.14. – | of the ground and the best manner of arranging for the clearing of wounded. The wounded received yesterday and today all belong to the 57th Rifles and 129th Baluchis. | for the clearing of wounded. SMM – |
| 25.10.14. – GROOTE VIERSTRAAT. | More quiet today. Despatched today 2 wounded and 8 sick. – In evening went round line of trenches of 129th Baluchis at Hollebeke and of 57th Rifles at OOSTTAVERNE & WYTSCHAETE. Received today 13 wounded & 2 sick – SMM. | Clearing hospital at Hazebrouck 11 wounded and 8 sick. SMM. |
| 26.10.14. – GROOTE VIERSTRAAT. | Busy day. – moved out at 3 k.m. for general action. 57th Rifles & 129th Baluchis were engaged. – Despatched today to Clearing hospital at BAILLEUL 5 sick – 8 wounded and 3 sick. – Stationed Bearer subdivisions at Hollebeke, OOSTTAVERNE and WYTSCHAETE. The 9th Bhopal Infantry have been detached from the Brigade and marched today to rejoin Headquarters Lahore Division. | The Connaught Rangers brought in 17 wounded. SMM. |

**WAR DIARY**
or
**INTELLIGENCE SUMMARY**

Army Form C. 2118.

28

| Hour, Date, Place. | Summary of Events and Information. | Remarks and references to Appendices. |
|---|---|---|
| 27.10.14. GROOTE VIERSTRAAT | Out again today expecting a general action and air raid. Brought in wounded from HOLLEBEKE, OOSTTAVERNE and WYTSCHAETE. Transferred by motor lorries to Clearing Hospital at BAILLEUL 45 wounded and 2 sick. Weather keeps extraordinarily fine and this not very cold. BMK | Admitted 40 wounded |
| 28.10.14. GROOTE VIERSTRAAT | A lull in the fighting today. Transferred 1 wounded & 2 sick to Clearing Hospital. Very fine day. BMK | Admitted 4 sick 10 wounded |
| 29.10.14. Groote Vierstraat | Groze shortly last night. Cloudy, raw & cold today with some wind. Rather heavy fighting in afternoon & evening. Admitted 17 wounded and 3 sick today. Transferred 15 wounded to A.2.15 Indian Clearing Hospital at Bailleul. O election of my F.Amb. left me today with the M.O. B.C. headquarters to report the headquarters of the Lahore Division. Weather fine. BMK | |

**Army Form C. 2118.**

**WAR DIARY**
or
**INTELLIGENCE SUMMARY.**

(Erase heading not required.)

Instructions regarding War Diaries and Intelligence Summaries are contained in F.S. Regs., Part II, and the Staff Manual respectively. Title pages will be prepared in manuscript.

29.

| Hour, Date, Place. | Summary of Events and Information. | Remarks and references to Appendices. |
|---|---|---|
| 30.10.1914 – GROOTE VIERSTRAAT | Very heavy fighting – I now have with me two complete tent subdivisions and 34 Bt of the Bearer Division of my field ambulance and I receive the wounded and sick of two Indian Infantry battalions, the 57th Rifles and 129th Baluchis which are divided up among four British Cavalry Brigades viz the 1st, 3rd, 4th & 5th. This wide scattering of them makes it difficult to collect them. Admitted 76 wounded and sick. Transferred to Clearing Hospital at Bailleul 7 wounded – weather fine. | |
| 31.10.14 – MILLE KRUIS – | Very heavy fighting – The Germans have made a most determined attack and have pushed our troops back a little – We have suffered heavy losses but all our men believe that the Germans have lost at least three times as heavily as we have – admitted 17 wounded and 1 sick – Transferred to No 15 Indian Clearing Hospital at Bailleul 86 wounded and 7 sick – In the course of nine days fighting in the trenches from the 23rd to the 31st October the 57th Rifles have lost 2 B.Os Killed 7 wounded and about 300 Indian ranks; the 129th Baluchis have lost 3 B.H Killed 3 wounded and about 250 rank & file (Indians) – Total I.B.Os killed wounded and about 550 Indian ranks out of the Indian battalion. (Signed) A. Cox? M.S. Cavalry? I.M.S.O. before they went into the trenches. | |

Gulab Singh & Sons, Calcutta—No. 22 Army C.—5-8-14—1,07,000.

No. 111 3d F.A.

(6414) Wt. W3906/P1607 2,500,000 7/18 McA & W Ltd (E 3591) Forms W3091/4.        Army Form W.3091.

# Cover for Documents.

---

**Nature of Enclosures.**

*Medicine & Phlebotomus.*

---

**Notes, or Letters written.**

No. 111 3rd F.A.

Nov. 1914

War Diary
No 111 Indian Field Ambulance

From 1st November 1914
to 30th November 1914

Volume I
30 / 6 / 36

Army Form C. 2118.

# WAR DIARY of No. 14 Indian Field Ambulance

## INTELLIGENCE SUMMARY.

(Erase heading not required.)

I.E. Force

Passed to Records. Sect<sup>n</sup>
on 11 - XII - 14

*GENERAL STAFF / WAR DIARIES / 10 DEC 1914 / BASE OFFICE INDIA*

No. 30.

| Hour, Date, Place. | Summary of Events and Information. | Remarks and references to Appendices. |
|---|---|---|
| 1.11.1914 – MILLEKRUIS to RENINGHELST | Very heavy fighting again today and again the Germans have pressed us back a little by sheer weight of superior numbers. Our losses have been heavy but the enemy has suffered losses about three times as great – Admitted 35 wounded and 1 sick – Transferred to Clearing Hospital at Bailleul. 11.15 Indian Clearing Hospital 33 wounded and 1 sick – CMT took 2 at I.M.S. Convey to III F.A. | |
| 2.11.1914 – RENINGHELST | Quiet day, Spent in collecting the scattered personnel of the 57 & Rifles and 129 th Baluchis – Admitted 10 wounded, no sick – Transferred to No 15 Indian Clearing Hospital at Bailleul. 3 men dangerously wounded – weather fine – The Germans have been driven back again from nearly all the ground they gained on the 31st Oct & 1st Nov. CMT | |
| 3.11.1914 – Reninghelst to STRAZEELE | Marched 10 miles – 7.45 a.m. to 1.30 p.m. – 10 miles – fine weather – The Motor Ambulances are most excellent vehicles for the transport of wounded – have not always been able to obtain them when I required them, but they are all invaluable troops to wounded men being transferred to the base – CMT Admitted 9 sick today – CMT | |

Army Form C. 2118.

# WAR DIARY
## or
## INTELLIGENCE SUMMARY.

(Erase heading not required.)

31.

| Hour, Date, Place. | Summary of Events and Information. | Remarks and references to Appendices. |
|---|---|---|
| 4.11.1914. STRAZEELE to ESTAIRES. | 6 miles - 10 A.M. to 11.40 A.M. - Weather very fine - Rejoined Headquarters of Lahore Division, and was rejoined by the detached portions of two sections of my F. Amb. under the command of Lieut. S. Kennedy J.M.S. and Lieut. A.H.C. Kirk J.M.S. - I learning today that Major W.H. Odium J.M.S. was transferred on the 2.11.1914 from No.111 I.F.A. to No.112 I.F.A. Admitted no sick or wounded - Transferring today 9 sick from Aug 16 to No.15 B.C. Hospital and 8 to No.112 I.F.A. GM | |
| 5.11.1914 - Estaires - | Half- Refitting - Not taking in wounded or sick today - | GM |
| 6.11.1914  " " | " " " " " " | GM |
| 7 & 10.11.1914 " " | " " " " " " | GM |
| 11.11.19.14. Estaires. | Reopened No. 111 I.F.A. today and sent out Bearer Division between Estaires & Rouge Croix. Station half-way between Estaires - Neuve Chapelle Road and by night at Rendezvous at Rouge Croix. The weather extraordinarily fine hitherto for this time of year, has now broken badly - rain & gale of wind having set in to-day - GM | |

# WAR DIARY
## INTELLIGENCE SUMMARY.

Army Form C. 2118.

32.

| Hour, Date, Place. | Summary of Events and Information. | Remarks and references to Appendices. |
|---|---|---|
| 12.11.1914. ESTAIRES | Rain, wind, mud, cold. Very severe weather for troops fighting & in trenches. 18 wounded were received in my F. Ambulance today. Of these 17 were transferred to No 15 Indian Clearing Hospital at Merville, and one, a Sepoy of the 59th Rifles shot through the brain, died. | EMM |
| 13.11.1914. | Severe weather continues. 13 wounded were admitted today. Of these four were transferred to No 15 Indian Clearing Hospital at Merville. | EMM |
| 14.11.1914. | Severe weather. Two wounded were admitted today, and 8 wounded & one of the 34th Pioneers was admitted today, hit in the abdomen by a shrapnel bullet. | EMM |
| 15.11.1914. | Very severe weather: Rain, sleet, and a file of wind - very cold. 8 wounded were admitted today, and 10 wounded were transferred to No 15 I.C.H. at Merville. | EMM |
| 16.11.1914. | Severe weather continues. No sick or wounded received today. | EMM |
| 17.11.1914. | Marched from Estaires to PARADIS, six miles, south by west. | EMM |

Army Form C. 2118.

# WAR DIARY
## INTELLIGENCE SUMMARY.
*(Erase heading not required.)*

33.

| Hour, Date, Place. | Summary of Events and Information. | Remarks and references to Appendices. |
|---|---|---|
| Paradis. 18.11.14. | Very hard frost last night — Sepoy Naryan Singh, 57th Rifles, was admitted on the 13.11.14. Shot through the left hand — wound self-inflicted accidentally according to his own statement — He is still retained in my field ambulance pending instructions from Divisional Headquarters — BMr— | |
| 19.11.1914. | Very severe weather — about 6 in. of snow today — froze hard last night — BMr— | |
| 20.11.14. | Very severe weather — freezing hard day & night — BMr— | |
| 21.11.14. | Ice on ponds almost thick enough to bear skating — BMr— | |
| 22.11.14. | Ice on ponds quite thick enough to bear skating — BMr— | |
| 23.11.14. PARADIS to ESSARS | Heavy fighting — Received 73 wounded & 2 sick — collected by my own & a neighbouring heavy division from FESTUBERT & neighbourhood — Very severe weather, threatening to snow — BMr— | |
| 24.11.14. ESSARS. | Very cold but thawing — Collected & admitted 12 wounded & 2 sick (Indians) also 2 sick British (soldiers, men of the Connaught Rangers. Transferred to Clearing Hospital 83 wounded and 4 sick. Visited the regimental aid posts and the trenches of the 57th Rifles and 129th Baluchis today at 4 ESTUBERT. BMr— | |

Army Form C. 2118.

# WAR DIARY
## — or —
## INTELLIGENCE SUMMARY.
(Erase heading not required.)

34.

| Hour, Date, Place. | Summary of Events and Information. | Remarks and references to Appendices. |
|---|---|---|
| 25.11.1914.<br>ESSARS to CHATEAU GORRE – 2 miles – | Still very cold, but trains continue. Collected and admitted 65 wounded and 50 sick Indians, also 1 wounded & 6 sick British soldiers, also 5 wounded German soldiers of 112th Infantry Regiment. Marched from Essars to Chateau Gorre, the latter being more commodious, more convenently placed and more suitable in every way. Transferred to clearing hospital 53 wounded and 1 sick Indian, and 6 wounded German soldiers. Also 1 wounded British soldier. Six sick British soldiers were transferred to No 7 British Field Ambulance. Lieut. A.H.C. Hill, I.M.S., was detached from my Fd. Amb. for temporary duty with the 129th Baluchis. JMM | |
| 26.11.1914.<br>Chateau Gorre. | One of the British soldiers brought in to me yesterday was a man of the 1st Connaught Rangers who was dug in in the line on the 23rd and lay in snow between the German trenches & ours for 48 hours without food or drink. I fear he will lose his life. He is of course certainly and on leg & high fever. Thus continues and it is also end today. Collected 11 th field amb of activity 5 wounded & 55 sick. Transferred to clearing hospital 5 wounded & 4 sick also brought in one wounded British soldier. P.T.O. | |

# WAR DIARY

## INTELLIGENCE SUMMARY

Army Form C. 2118.

35.

| Hour, Date, Place. | Summary of Events and Information. | Remarks and references to Appendices. |
|---|---|---|
| 26.11.1914. Chateau Gorre | Transferred to Clearing Hospitals 1 British wounded soldier and 8 wounded + 14 sick Indians. This Chateau Gorre makes a most excellent place for a field ambulance; it is commodious, well lighted by electricity, convenient to the trenches from which the wounded are brought in, and readily accessible by good roads to the motor ambulances which carry away patients to the Clearing Hospital. There is no other building district in this district at all comparable to it in facilities & conveniences for bringing in, caring for and despatching to the base wounded & sick men. Visited the Regimental aid posts of the 9th Bhopals & 57th to the N of PLANTIN today. EMW | |
| 27.11.1914. Chateau Gorre | Collected from the field and admitted into my Fd. Ambulance; British 2 wounded + 2 sick; Indians 8 wounded + 34 sick. Transferred to Clearing Hospital 8 wounded + 36 sick Indians. Returned to their regiments for duty 23 Indians - viz 19 sick + 4 wounded. Mild winter weather, no rain. EMW | |
| 28.11.1914. Chateau Gorre | Collected + admitted Indians, 7 wounded + 18 sick; British, 8 sick. Transferred to Clearing Hospitals 2 British wounded and Indians 5 wounded + 11 sick. Discharged to duty with their corps 4 wounded + 32 sick Indians. Cold wind today. EMW | |

# WAR DIARY
## INTELLIGENCE SUMMARY.
*(Erase heading not required.)*

Army Form C. 2118.

36.

| Hour, Date, Place. | Summary of Events and Information. | Remarks and references to Appendices. |
|---|---|---|
| 2.11.1914 – Chateau Norre | Collected and admitted: British 5 sick, Indians 3 wounded and 37 sick – Transferred to Clearing hospital 3 sick & 4 wounded – Returned to their regiments for duty 4 wounded & 15 sick – Four sweepers of the 9th Bhopals were admitted into my Field Ambulance suffering from Carbon monoxide poisoning, caused by sleeping in a Cookhouse with a coal fire in a brazier – One of them died hovering between life & death – I have called the A.D.M.S., Lahore Division, to have a Divisional Order issued forbidding Warming all troops this danger, now that Coal is being issued for warming purposes to all troops in billets. – Two men of the 58th Rifles who were left out on the 23rd with more brought into my field ambulance this evening after lying out in the Open for Six days & nights – They were under the rifle fire of the German trenches at short range and unable to move and were not discovered until today – They were in surprisingly good condition considering the awful exposure they had been through, the ground was covered with deep snow all the first 24 hours of their exposure, even though it was thawing – I hope |  |

Army Form C. 2118.

37.

WAR DIARY
or
INTELLIGENCE SUMMARY.

(Erase heading not required.)

Instructions regarding War Diaries and Intelligence Summaries are contained in F. S. Regs., Part II, and the Staff Manual respectively. Title pages will be prepared in manuscript.

| Hour, Date, Place. | Summary of Events and Information. | Remarks and references to Appendices. |
|---|---|---|
| 30.11.1914. CHATEAU GORRE | Collected & received 3 wounded British soldiers, belonging to the Leicester Regiment. One of them died, his legs having been blown to pieces by a German bomb in the trenches. Also collected & received on my British officer and 21 sick and six wounded Indians. Transferring to clearing hospital 10 sick & 5 wounded Indians, and returned to duty with their regiment 6 sick & 2 wounded Indians. Weather mild & fine. During the month of November 1914 I collected and received on myself ambulance 11 wounded British soldiers, belonging to the Royal Artillery, Black Watch, Connaught Rangers, Lincoln Regt., Leicester Regt. & 1 1/25 British soldiers belonging to the R.A., Connaught Rangers, Leicester Regt. and Army Service Corps, and five wounded Indians soldiers belonging to the 112th Infantry. My figures for admissions of Indians during the month of November are 323 wounded and 262 sick. There has been no undue prevalence of disease. In consequence of the very severe weather with snow & hard frost, there were a good many cases of frost-bite. A. M. Frost Lt. Col. I.M.S. Comdg N.M.F.A. | |

Gulab Singh & Sons, Calcutta.—No. 22 Army.—5-8-14—1,07,000.

No. 111 2nd E. F. A.

(6392) Wt. W6192/P875 1,500,000 4/18 McA & W Ltd (E 2815) Forms W3091/4.     Army Form W.3091.

# Cover for Documents.

### Nature of Enclosures.

M E D I C I N E.

7. ~~RELAPSING, TICK & PHLEBOTOMUS FEVERS.~~

---

### Notes, or Letters written.

Warburg
No. 111 Indian Field Ambulance

From 1-12-14
To 31-12-14

Volume I
pp 376-48

Dec. 1914

# WAR DIARY

Army Form C. 2118.

**Confidential**

1/2/III Indian — Field Ambulance — 3?

INTELLIGENCE SUMMARY.

(Erase heading not required.)

ADJUTANT GENERAL INDIA
-3 JAN 1915
BASE OFFICE

| Hour, Date, Place. | Summary of Events and Information. | Remarks and references to Appendices. |
|---|---|---|
| 1.12.1914. CHATEAU GORRE | Weather mild & fine – East strong wind blowing – Collected and received 8 wounded British soldiers, 1 Officer R.F.A., 1 Black Watch, and Connaught Rangers 1 – Also 11 wounded & 30 sick Indians – Transferred to Clearing Hospital 6 wounded & 3 sick Indians – Returned to duty with their regiments 2 wounded & 4 sick Indians. Two sweepers of the 9th Bhopal Infantry were poisoned by Carbonic Acid on the 29.11.14 in consequence of sleeping in a closed room with a brazier burning coal in the middle of it, died this morning. The A.D.M.S. has on duty Inspector had a Lahore Divisional orderly published warning all units against this danger. C.M.R. Proof. Lt.Col. I.M.S. (On 29.9.1914 B.A.) | |
| 2.12.1914. | Strong wind blowing – cold – Collected & received 6 wounded British soldiers, all of the Black Watch – also 4 wounded & 24 sick Indians – Transferred to Clearing Hospital 9 wounded & 28 sick Indians, and one British Officer. Returned to duty with their Corps 3 sick Indians – C.M.R. Visited the regimental aid posts at La Plantin this Afternoon – 9th Bhopal Infantry, 98 th Goorkhas, Black Watch re– C.M.R. | |

# WAR DIARY
## INTELLIGENCE SUMMARY.

Army Form C. 2118.

38

| Hour, Date, Place. | Summary of Events and Information. | Remarks and references to Appendices. |
|---|---|---|
| 3.12.1914. CHATEAU GORRE | Gale of wind from the west, cold. Collecting & received 7 wounded & 4 sick British Ullan, 1 of of the Black Watch, Connaught Rangers, Seaforth Highlanders, R.F.A., and Leicester Regt., also 12 wounded & 23 sick Indians. Transferred to Clearing Hospital 7 wounded & 23 sick Indians. Returned to duty with their regiments 40 sick & 2 wounded Indians. | |
| 4.12.1914. Chateau Gorre to HINGETTES. | Gale of wind from the east - very cold - Rain & hail Transferred to Clearing Hospital 5 wounded & 35 sick Indians. Returned to duty with their regiments 10 sick Indians. Marched from Chateau Gorre to Hingettes, 6 miles. YMK. | |
| 8.12.14. HINGETTES. | In accordance with sanction contained in A.A.G. No 817-A of 5. XII.14. 11nd G.H. Frost IMS reported his departure on ten days leave. Capt. C.A. Rankin IMS. [illegible] in command of his Field Ambulance during his absence | CARankin Capt IMS |

Gulab Singh & Sons, Calcutta—No. 22 Army C.—5-8-14—1,07,000.

Army Form C. 2118.

App. 39

# WAR DIARY
## or
## INTELLIGENCE SUMMARY.
*(Erase heading not required.)*

| Hour, Date, Place. | Summary of Events and Information. | Remarks and references to Appendices. |
|---|---|---|
| 10. XII. 14<br>HINGETTE<br>to<br>HALTE | Visit ADMS to 145 of 10th XII/14 marched at 3.40 pm from HINGETTE to HALTE 4 mile to billets. Early occupied by No 112 J.F.A. & prepared to pave for the reception of sick. Waggon trouble en route, owing to no oven-stuff as the men had in being unprepared & hospital comforts accumulated trash to trunk & gramme Serenity, but our transport-reserves the same. Under ADMS, No 920 of 10th XII/14 at A. KENNEDY was this day transferred to No 112 J.F.A. for temporary duty. Ambulance Waggon provided at 8.30 am to ESSARS. CROIX DE FER, LE HAMEL, GORRE & LETOURET to collect sick. |  |
| 11. XII. 14 | Under orders from ADMS No 1864 recd at 6 pm conveying 6 Waggons 24 stretchers 96 bearers & nurse & Wardorder to Scluinj surgeon marched at 3.30 am then morning with transport to a railway waggon on the Rue de Bethune through him at 5 am to act in accord to the Forsue Division of No 113 J.F.A. in the French lotly loss |  |

Gulab Singh & Sons, Calcutta—No. 22 Army C.—5.8.14—1,07,900.

# WAR DIARY
## INTELLIGENCE SUMMARY

Army Form C. 2118.

40

| Hour, Date, Place. | Summary of Events and Information. | Remarks and references to Appendices. |
|---|---|---|
| HALTE. 16. XII. 14 | Lt. A. Kennedy rejoined battery from temporary duty with No 112 Q.F.A. Lt Anderson & the Bearer Division remained at the rendezvous in the RUE DE BETHUNE all temporary - they transported 35 Sick from the 125th Napier Rifles & 6 113 1/2 A at CHATEAU GORRE at 11 am. | |
| 1.30 p.m. | Regt installed had connection with - 1st Aid posts of the 1/4 Rifle Brig, 57 Rifles, FF & 47 Sikhs. There were no casualties in the 4/3 Sikhs two in the 6/R & twenty four in the 129 Baluchis including one British (Prev - this latter all transfers) to the call division at HALTE receiving these at 6-30pm. a further sixteen wounded from the 3 and Sirmur received 15 Gurk division at 10 pm and a long continued of 4 waggons & twenty four wounded has been brought in which had been driven by Lt Anderson reached at 2-15 am. The work of the last division was carried on by Capt Rendall & Lt Kennedy. | |
| 17 . XII . 14 | One of the wounded died in the waggon en route to HALTE & another died shortly after admission. Twelve wounded were evacuated during the night to Clearing hospital by a timely convoy of Motor Ambulances. | |

# WAR DIARY

## INTELLIGENCE SUMMARY.

Army Form C. 2118.

47.

(Erase heading not required.)

| Hour, Date, Place. | Summary of Events and Information. | Remarks and references to Appendices. |
|---|---|---|
| HALTE, 17.XII.14 | Forty three were wounded, of whom 22 were lying down cases & two sick were evacuated this morning at 10 a.m. Eight wounded remaining for evacuation. Since 2 p.m. yesterday afternoon thirteen Dinisers the field ambulances under Lt Anderson carried another ~~to evac~~ 65 ~~Dinior~~ wounded, of whom 30 were lying-down cases. Owing to the situation of the advposts & the marshy nature of the country round & the bad condition of the roads, the bearers had to carry patients for a mile to get in to the ambulance waggons. The bearer Division was out for 23 hours & Lt Anderson reports that they worked my well & highly commends the work of S.A.S. Hokum Singh & 508 Haggardu Singh. SAS Karta Ram also worked well. I am of opinion that the successful ~~case~~ collection & transport of the large numbers of severely wounded men, under considerable difficulties, to a tent Division five miles away, is mainly due to the initiative and resource of Lt Z.J. Anderson I.M.S. During the night of 16th/17th Dec the Tut Division evacuated 65 wounded Indian soldiers & 1 British officer. 58 of them by Mawr on 17 Dec to Clearing Hospital |  |

# WAR DIARY
## INTELLIGENCE SUMMARY.
(Erase heading not required.)

Army Form C. 2118.

42.

| Hour, Date, Place. | Summary of Events and Information. | Remarks and references to Appendices. |
|---|---|---|
| 17.XII.14 | Under orders from ADMS to 18th of the date Lt HILL M.D. was transferred to Nos 129th Batteries for temporary duty vice Lt PATON who was sick. Lt HILL proceeded to join the 129th at 6 p.m. | |
| HALTE — 1½ miles short of BETHUNE on road to LOCON. 18.12.1914 | Lt. Col. G.H. Frost, I.M.S., having reported last evening from ten days leave to England, has resumed command of No 111 F.A., the three officers present being Capt. G.H. Reinhold, I.M.S., Lieut. F.J. Anderson, I.M.S., and Lieut. A. Kennedy, I.M.S. — Rain + wind, not very cold, very little sickness among the troops. — Admitted 3 sick Indian followers. — EMF. 2nd R.W.K.R. & 1/4th K.R.R. | |
| 19.12.1914. Halte | Rain + wind, not very cold, singularly little sickness among the troops. No admission today, 8 sick transferred to Clearing Hospital. EMF | |
| 20.12.1914. Halte. | Rain + wind — very cold at night — admitted 83 wounded and 99 sick Indian soldiers. Also two sick British Officers — Major B.M.R. Brockhurst, 1/4th Gorkhas, and Lieut. J.A. Balfour, 1st K.R.R., both suffering from rheumatism. Despatched to Clearing Hospital 39 wounded + 87 sick Indian Soldiers. Returned on duty with his regiment — EMF | |

Army Form C. 2118.

# WAR DIARY
## INTELLIGENCE SUMMARY.
*(Erase heading not required.)*

Instructions regarding War Diaries and Intelligence Summaries are contained in F. S. Regs., Part II, and the Staff Manual respectively. Title pages will be prepared in manuscript.

| Hour, Date, Place. | Summary of Events and Information. | Remarks and references to Appendices. |
|---|---|---|
| HALTE - 21.12.1914. | Rain & wind - very cold - Most trying conditions in the Trenches, especially near Le Plantin, where they are half full of water and liquid / mud : at that place they have dug a well from 2 to 3 feet of water in them - Admitted 101 wounded and 48 sick Indian soldiers - Transferred to Clearing Hospital the two British officers admitted yesterday, and 123 wounded & 57 sick Indian soldiers - Subadar Sub Lal A Ranti and one Rifleman of the 1/9.R., and a daffadar of the 34th Poona Horse died today and were buried in the paddock opposite the ambulance - | 48. |
| 22.12.1914. | Rain & wind, very cold. No admission today - Transferred 5 wounded Indian soldiers to Clearing Hospital - The Bearer Division of my Field Ambulance was constantly at work from 3 P.m. on the 20th to 12 midnight 21-22.12.14, at Chateau Farre and two miles in front of Chateau Farre at Festubert and Le Plantin close to our trenches, clearing wounded from the regiments of Sirhind, dressing & carrying for them, and sending them into the Court. | |

Army Form C. 2118.

# WAR DIARY
## INTELLIGENCE SUMMARY.
(Erase heading not required.)

4th

| Hour, Date, Place. | Summary of Events and Information. | Remarks and references to Appendices. |
|---|---|---|

HALTE, 22.12.1914.

Division at Halte – Lieut. F. J. Anderson, I.M.S., was in command of the Bearer Division, and did excellent work, as he has so often done before in this war, at Chateau Gorre, Festubert & Plantin – M1116, 1st Class Sub. asst. Surgeon, Rajindar Singh, I.S.M.D., also did most useful work during the period. I myself saw him, during the night of the 25th at Le Plantin, close to our trenches, where there was a heavy attack in progress, with plenty of bullets & shells flying about, working admirably well and rendering most useful assistance in the regimental aid posts.

Capt. C. A. Reinhold, I.M.S., a thoroughly capable Officer in every respect and an uncommonly skilful surgeon, worked strenuously well in the tent division on the 20 & 21.12.1914, dealing in a most efficient manner with no less than 184 wounded and 145 sick Indian soldiers in these two days – He has performed most valuable & distinguished service of the same kind on several other occasions when there was a heavy

# WAR DIARY
## INTELLIGENCE SUMMARY.
*(Erase heading not required.)*

Army Form C. 2118.

Remarks and references to Appendices. 46.

| Hour, Date, Place. | Summary of Events and Information. |
|---|---|
| HALTE – 22.12.1914. | Pressure of wounded too deal with rapidly & on short notice – particularly at Groote Vierstraat near YPRES when he administered surgical aid most ably to 235 wounded in ten days with very poor accommodation for them in barns, and yet with highly successful results, the period being from the 23rd October to the 1st November; again during the five days 23rd to 27th November, at Brasan & Chateau Gore, when he dealt cleverly & successfully with 163 wounded and 146 sick Indians, besides 15 sick & wounded British soldiers and 5 wounded Germans, and again on the 16th Dec. at Halte when he dressed and despatched to the Clearing hospital 65 wounded Indian Soldiers and 1 wounded British Officer – This is a fine record of good work, skillfully & most successfully performed under difficult circumstances and deserves full & careful attention. – SMC |

# WAR DIARY
## INTELLIGENCE SUMMARY

Army Form C. 2118.

(Erase heading not required.)

| Hour, Date, Place. | Summary of Events and Information. | Remarks and references to Appendices. |
|---|---|---|
| 23.12.1914. HALTE to LOZINGHEM | A little rain and a little snow – Marched to LOZINGHEM about 10 miles and took up billets near headquarters of the Lahore Division – The whole of the Lahore Division has now come out of the trenches for a rest, the withdrawal having commenced on the 21.12.14, evening – admitted 1 sick Indian follower – GMM | |
| LOZINGHEM. 24.12.1914. | Fine day – Began to freeze in the evening – Admitted 14 sick Indian soldiers – GMM | |
| 25.12.1914 – | Froze hard last night, and all today – White Christmas – Admitted 81 sick holiday soldiers – Transferred to Clearing Hospital 1 wounded & 15 sick – Returned to their regiments 4 sick & 15 wounded. GMM | |
| 26.12.1914 – | Froze hard last night, before to thaw this morning – Admitted 1 wounded & 87 sick Indian Ranks – Transferred to Clearing Hospital 46 sick & 1 wounded & returned to their regiments 1 wounded & 1 sick & 1 boy. GMM | |

**WAR DIARY**
or
**INTELLIGENCE SUMMARY.**

Army Form C. 2118.

48.

(Erase heading not required.)

| Hour, Date, Place. | Summary of Events and Information. | Remarks and references to Appendices. |
|---|---|---|
| DZINGHEM 27.12.1914. | Rain — Heavy gale of wind — Hail showers — Admitted 20 sick & two soldiers — Transferred to Clearing Hospital 2 wounded & 83 sick — 1 Army Bearer died of pneumonia. My field ambulance is taking in all the sick (Indians) of the Lahore Division since the 23rd inst. — to the date orderers and sick followers. My hospital accommodation is so limited here — only two small rooms in which I cannot keep any more than 32 sick at a time — that I am obliged to transfer patients at once to the Clearing Hospital when large numbers come to be treated — I have therefore asked the A.D.M.S. of the Division to call upon Medical officers of regiments to retain under their own care as long as possible slight cases likely to be able to return to duty soon. This is feasible as regiments are now out of the trenches & resting in billets — NWM — | |
| 28.12.14 — | Rain, wind, cold — Admitted 1 wounded & 19 sick — The wounded man is a Havildar of the 4th Gowrkhas who was shot accidentally through the right thigh by a pistol — Transferred to Clearing Hospital 1 wounded and 17 sick — NWM — | |

Army Form C. 2118.

# WAR DIARY
## INTELLIGENCE SUMMARY
(Erase heading not required.)

48

Instructions regarding War Diaries and Intelligence Summaries are contained in F. S. Regs., Part II, and the Staff Manual respectively. Title pages will be prepared in manuscript.

| Hour, Date, Place. | Summary of Events and Information. | Remarks and references to Appendices. |
|---|---|---|
| LOZINGHEM. 29.12.1914. | High wind, much rain, cold. - Admitted 9 sick - Clearing Hospital 12 sick. - Returned 1 sick man to his regiment - | Transferred to his regiment - BMc - |
| 30.12.14. - | Fine cold winter day. - Admitted 17 sick - Hospital 11 sick. - | Transferred to Clearing BMc - Capt. R.C.H. Reinhold, I.M.S., reported his departure this morning on 7 days leave to England. BMc |
| 31.12.14. | Rain & wind - cold. - Admitted 13 sick Indian soldiers - Transferred to Clearing Hospital 16 sick. - Up to this time there has been very little sickness among Indian troops, of a serious character, with the exception of cases of frost-bite due to hardship and exposure to cold and wet in the trenches. - | |

BMcBrook, Lt. Col. I.M.S.
Com dg N° 111 Indian Field Ambulance -

# WAR DIARY

## OF

### No. III. Indian Field Ambulance.

From 1st January 1915 To 31st January 1915

(Confidential.) of Major G.H. Grove, I.M.S.

# WAR DIARY

**Instructions** regarding War Diaries and Intelligence Summaries are contained in F. S. Regs., Part II. and the Staff Manual respectively. Title pages will be prepared in manuscript.

Army Form C. 2118
A. G's Office at Base
Passed to S. Sect"
on 18 - 2 - 15
I. E. Force
No. 3 Section

## INTELLIGENCE SUMMARY

Comd of the Indian Field Ambulance –
(Erase heading not required.)
Volume V

Summary of Events and Information from 1.1.1915 to 31.1.1915.

| Hour, Date, Place. | | Remarks and references to Appendices. |
|---|---|---|
| LOZINGHEM 1.1.1915 | | Rain, wind, cold. Admitted 13 sick Indian soldiers – Transferred 11 sick to Clearing Hospital – Returned two men to duty with their regiments. I admitted to mention, until now that N° 2419 A.B. Mahomed Hasan, N° 2 Coy, A.B. Corps, was wounded near Le Plantin during the night of the 20-21.10.1914 while out with the Reserve Division, under the command of Lieut. A. Kennedy, I.M.S., collecting wounded. His wound was a bullet wound through the leg – bones being broken – G.H. Moore. Lt. Col. I.M.S. Com dg N° 1 I.F.A. |
| 2.1.15. | | Rain & wind – not very cold – Admitted 19 sick, transferred 14 to Clearing Hospital, and returned two to duty with their regiments – GHM |
| 3.1.15. | | Rain – not cold – Admitted 15 sick, transferred 14 to Clearing Hospital and returned 1 man to duty with his regiment – GHM |

# WAR DIARY

## INTELLIGENCE SUMMARY.

*(Erase heading not required.)*

Army Form C. 2118.

51.

| Hour, Date, Place. | Summary of Events and Information | Remarks and references to Appendices. |
|---|---|---|
| LOZINGHEM 4.1.15. | Rain + wind – not cold – Admitted 19 sick transferred 17 to Clearing Hospital – One man, a driver of No 2 B.F. ambulance died in Hospital from pneumonia. | EMM |
| 5.1.15. | Rain + wind – not cold – Admitted 18 sick, transferred 24 to Clearing Hospital + returned 4 men to their regiments. | EMM |
| 6.1.1915 – | Rain + wind – not cold – Admitted 17 sick, transferred 14 to Clearing Hospital 7 and returned 2 men to duty with their regiments – Experience shows that the Tent lanterns supplied to this Field ambulance in India as part of its equipment are very heavy, give a very poor light and are of bad design + easily get broken. J ordinary hurricane lanterns made by Hinks, Wells, Smith or other good makers would be better in every respect than the present tent lanterns – EMM | |
| 7.1.15 – | Rain + wind – not cold – Admitted 5 sick, transferred 3, also admitted today and transferred to clearing Hospital Major General P. McCracken, C.B. i.e. Infantry Bde. EMM who got frost-bitten in his feet during the heavy fighting near Armentry 20 to 22. 12.14 | EMM |

# WAR DIARY

## INTELLIGENCE SUMMARY.

*(Erase heading not required.)*

Army Form C. 2118.

52.

| Hour, Date, Place. | Summary of Events and Information. | Remarks and references to Appendices. |
|---|---|---|
| LOZINGHEM — 8.1.15. | Rain & wind — not cold — Admitted 14 sick, Clearing Hospital — GMW— | transferred 11 to |
| 9.1.15. | Rain & wind — not cold — Admitted 13 sick, transferred 8 — returned to duty 1 — GMW— | |
| 10.1.15. | Fine Bright sunny day — the first day this thing for a long time — Admitted 12 sick, transferred 8 — The cases of mumps today just now, and for some time past, respiratory diseases, especially bronchitis, have been the most notable cause of admissions to hospital — A few cases of pneumonia have occurred, not many. Some of the returns to sent from India to fill gaps in regiments that have been in August have been found unfit in consequence of age & debility, piles, varicose veins &c to perform the ordinary work required of soldiers in the trenches in this war. — GMW | |

Army Form C. 2118.

# WAR DIARY
## INTELLIGENCE SUMMARY.
*(Erase heading not required.)*

| Hour, Date, Place. | Summary of Events and Information. | Remarks and references to Appendices. |
|---|---|---|
| LOZINGHEM 11.1.1915. | Rain & wind last night following a fine day yesterday - Weather was fine this morning but broke down badly in the afternoon - admitted 15 sick, transferred 20, died 1 (Broncho-pneumonia, a havildar of the 15th Sikhs) - GMM - | |
| 12.1.15. | Rain & wind - not very cold - admitted 19 sick, transferred 16 to Clearing Hospital - GMM - 2 cases of mumps are among admissions today. GMM - | |
| 13.1.15. | Rain & wind - Rather cold - admitted 31 sick, transferred 28 to Lahore Clearing Station - GMM - | |
| 14.1.15. | Rain & wind - Rather cold - admitted 45 sick, including one case mumps - Discharged 2 to duty. Transferred 43 to Lahore Clearing Station - GMM - | |
| 15.1.15. | Rain & wind - Cold - admitted 1 officer, Capt. C.H. Reinhold, R.M.S. and 52. NCOs. Discharged 5 to duty. Transferred 50 to Lahore Clearing Station. GMM - | |

Army Form C. 2118.

# WAR DIARY
## INTELLIGENCE SUMMARY.
*(Erase heading not required.)*

Instructions regarding War Diaries and Intelligence Summaries are contained in F. S. Regs., Part II, and the Staff Manual respectively. Title pages will be prepared in manuscript.

| Hour, Date, Place. | Summary of Events and Information. | Remarks and references to Appendices. |
|---|---|---|
| LOZINGHEM 16.1.1915. | Rain & wind, cold. - Admitted 1 Officer, (Capt. R.B. Meiklh, 5th Rifles,) and 22 men. - Transferred to Lahore Clearing Station 2 Officers and 18 men. - SMF. | |
| 17.1.15. | Rain, cold. - Admitted 5 sick. - Transferred 13. - SMF. | |
| 18.1.15. | Rain, cold. Admitted 53 sick, including one case of mumps. Discharged one man to duty. Transferred 13 to Lahore Clearing Station. - SMF. | |
| 19.1.15. | Rain, cold. - Admitted 4 sick (including Sub. Ass. Surgeon Kaubaiya Lal to own field ambulance). - Discharged 10 to duty. Transferred 11 to Lahore Clearing Station. - SMF. | |
| 20.1.15. | Admitted 4. Transferred none. - The large numbers admitted between the 13th & 18th inst. were due to the fact that two brigades of the division (the Sirhind & Jullundur Brigades) were moved into (the Trenches) and had to send in men (nearly) severely in the hope of obtaining an early cure. - The majority of these | |

Gulab Singh & Sons, Calcutta—No. 22 Army C.—5-8-14—4,07,000.

# WAR DIARY
## INTELLIGENCE SUMMARY.
*(Erase heading not required.)*

Army Form C. 2118.

| Hour, Date, Place. | Summary of Events and Information. | Remarks and references to Appendices. |
|---|---|---|
| LOZINGHEM. 20.1.1915. | Casualties were due to dizziness of the respiratory system provoked by the wet cold weather which they felt acutely. Besides this a certain proportion of men recently arrived from India as re-inforcements were found to be physically unfit for active service in the field under the arduous conditions now being experienced — GMC — | 552 |
| 21.1.15. | Admitted 15. Transferred 9. Weather cold but dry — GMC — | |
| 22.1.15. | Admitted 5. Transferred 6. Weather cold but dry — GMC — | |
| 23.1.15. | Admitted 16, including one case of modified small-pox, which occurred in a man of the 15th Sikhs, who arrived with a batch of re-inforcements. Colonel A. B. Hudson, A.D.M.S. Lahore Division, is also admitted today suffering from pyrexia. Discharged 2 men to duty and transferred 9 to Clearing Station. The men admitted which have had been vaccinated previously — GMC — They were admitted for observation to these mity quarters & to Base General Hospital at Boulogne. He was transferred | |

# WAR DIARY or INTELLIGENCE SUMMARY.

Army Form C. 2118.

56.

(Erase heading not required.)

| Hour, Date, Place. | Summary of Events and Information. | Remarks and references to Appendices. |
|---|---|---|
| LOZINGHEM. 24.1.1915. | Admitted 21; discharged to duty 3; Transferred 10. | Cold + dry – BMR. |
| 25.1.15. | Admitted 16, including 3 cases of mumps; discharged to duty 2; Transferred 3. Cases of mumps are transferred to the Lahore Casualty Clearing Station. The name "Casualty Clearing Station" has just recently been substituted for the name "Clearing Hospital." | BMR. |
| 26.1.15. | Froze last night – a light sprinkling of snow. Admitted 40, including two cases of mumps; discharged to duty 6; Transferred to Casualty Clearing Station 2. Capt. F.C. Boyd J.M.S. has been admitted today for debility after influenza. | BMR. |
| 27.1.15. | Admitted 32, including 3 cases of mumps; discharged to duty 9; Transferred 36. Colonel G.R. Hoghton A.D.M.S., Lahore Division, admitted for fever F.U.O. Dr. 2 3.1.15 has been transferred today to No. 4 Casualty Clearing Station. | BMR. |

Army Form C. 2118.

# WAR DIARY
## or
## INTELLIGENCE SUMMARY.

*(Erase heading not required.)*

57-

Instructions regarding War Diaries and Intelligence Summaries are contained in F.S. Regs., Part II, and the Staff Manual respectively. Title pages will be prepared in manuscript.

| Hour, Date, Place. | Summary of Events and Information. | Remarks and references to Appendices. |
|---|---|---|
| LOZINGHEM 28.1.15.- | Cold & damp - admitted 36, including 1 case of mumps; discharged to duty 2; Transferred 2 to Casualty Clearing Station (Lahore) Capt. T. E. Boyd, 9.M.S., N°110 9.F. Ambulance, admitted on the 26.1.15 for debility after influenza, has been Transferred to-day to N°4 Casualty Clearing Station - RMr- | |
| 29.1.15.- | Cold & damp - admitted 84, including two cases of mumps; discharged to duty 13; Transferred to Lahore Casualty Clearing Station 37 - RMr- | |
| 30.1.15.- | Cold & damp - admitted 91, including 4 cases of mumps & 3 queries; discharged to duty 19; transferred 66. Major P. L. Swifte, 57th Rifles, has been admitted to-day and transferred to N°4 Casualty Clearing Station - disease chronic rheumatism - RMr- | |
| | P.T.O. RMr- | |

Gulab Singh & Sons, Calcutta—No. 22 Army C.—5-8-14—1,07,000.

Army Form C. 2118.

# WAR DIARY
## INTELLIGENCE SUMMARY.
(Erase heading not required.)

Instructions regarding War Diaries and Intelligence Summaries are contained in F. S. Regs., Part II, and the Staff Manual respectively. Title pages will be prepared in manuscript.

| Hour, Date, Place. | Summary of Events and Information. | Remarks and references to Appendices. |
|---|---|---|
| LOZINGHEM to LA MIQUELLERIE 31.1.1915. | Marched today to new billets at La MIQUELLERIE in Ferozepore Brigade area – marched with the Ferozepore Brigade. Country (i.e. the 9th Infantry, 125th Rifles, 109th Baluchis and 98th Gurkha Rifles. Very bad weather – snow-storm in the middle of the day – started to work on the march – Distance of march 9 miles, time 11.30 a.m. to 2.30 p.m. I found very good billets for a field ambulance at La Miquellerie in the house if the Maire of Busnes (BUSNES) – Admitted 1. Transferred 84 to No.112 I.F.A. at LOZINGHEM. During the whole of the month of January and the last eight days of December No.111 I.F.A. has been taking in all the Indian sick of the whole of the Lahore Division; it has now been allotted to the Ferozepore Brigade area, and will in future take in the sick of the Ferozepore Brigade only. – E.M.Wrench. Lt. Col. I.M.S. Comdg No.111 I.F.A. | S.8. |

121/4/19.
Feb. 1915.

121/4/19

Serial No. 153

# WAR DIARY
## OF
No. III Indian Field Ambulance.

From 1st February 1915 to 28th February 1915

Confidential –

**WAR DIARY**

of Lieut. Colonel J. H. Spratt, I.M.S.,
Commanding 23rd Indian Field Ambulance. P. 59. –
and S.M.O. Ferozepore Brigade –

**INTELLIGENCE SUMMARY.**

Army Form C. 2118.

Vol. VI

From 1.2.1915. to 28.2.1915.

| Hour, Date, Place. | Summary of Events and Information. | Remarks and references to Appendices. |
|---|---|---|
| BASE OFFICE LA MIQUELLERIE 1.2.1915. | Cold & damp – Admitted 15 – None transferred or discharged. I have now been appointed S.M.O., Ferozepore Brigade in addition to my other duties. – | MMProb.Sh.L/Cpl.I.M.S. Com of No 111 F.A. – S.M.O. Ferozepore Brigade |
| 2.2.1915. | Cold & damp – Admitted 7, including one case of mumps; Transferred to Lahore Casualty Clearing Station 7. – | EMM |
| 3.2.15. – | Cold & damp – Admitted 5, including 1 case of mumps; discharged to duty 1; Transferred to C.C.S. 4. | EMM |
| 4.2.15. | Cold & wet – Admitted 8, Transferred to C.C.S. 6. | EMM |
| 5.2.15 – | Cold & damp – Admitted 6, including 1 case of mumps; discharged to duty 3, Transferred 4 to C.C.S. 1 case of mumps; discharged | EMM |

# WAR DIARY
## INTELLIGENCE SUMMARY.

*(Erase heading not required.)*

Army Form C. 2118
60.

| Hour, Date, Place. | Summary of Events and Information. | Remarks and references to Appendices. |
|---|---|---|
| LA MIQUELLERIE 6.2.15. | Admitted 10, discharged to duty 4, Transferred to Casualty Clearing Station 2. DMS | Transferred 7th Lahore DMS |
| 7.2.15. | Fine day, cloudy towards evening cold. Admitted 11, including 2 early 7th, discharged to duty 2; Transferred 8 to C.C.S. All drinking water is now ordered to be chlorinated on account of the suspicion of the existence of enteric fever in this district. All contacts of cases of measles, mumps are are segregated, and all infected billets are marked with the name of the infectious disease and the date of occurrence of the last case - DMS. An accurate & precise description of the infected house, to make it possible to identify it exactly is sent to the A.D.M.S., Lahore Division - DMS | |

# WAR DIARY

## INTELLIGENCE SUMMARY.

*(Erase heading not required.)*

Army Form C. 2118.

61.

| Hour, Date, Place. | Summary of Events and Information. | Remarks and references to Appendices. |
|---|---|---|
| L.A.M.! QUELLER 8.2.1915. | Cold & damp. Admitted 3, including one case of mumps. Transferred 1 to Lahore Casualty Clearing Station. Admitted Lt. Col. A. Grant Comdt. 2/8 G.R., for dislocation of the internal semi-lunar fibro-cartilage, right knee, the result of an accident. BMM. | |
| 9.2.15. | Very bad weather - rient wind - Admitted 9 including one case of mumps and 5 of measles. Discharged to duty 2. Transferred to C.C.S. 12. Also transferred Lt. Col. A. Grant, 2/8 G.R. to No 4 C.C.S. BMM. | |
| 10.2.15. | Fine bright day. Admitted 8, including 4 cases of mumps, discharged to duty 1; transferred to C.C.S. The 3rd City of London Territorial Regiment joined the Ferozepore Brigade today. BMM. | |

Army Form C. 2118.

# WAR DIARY
## INTELLIGENCE SUMMARY.
(Erase heading not required.)

62.

Instructions regarding War Diaries and Intelligence Summaries are contained in F. S. Regs., Part II, and the Staff Manual respectively. Title pages will be prepared in manuscript.

| Hour, Date, Place. | Summary of Events and Information. | Remarks and references to Appendices. |
|---|---|---|
| LA MIQUELLERIE 11.2.15. | Frost last night, bright sunny morning, cold cloudy with rain in evening. Admitted 5, including 1 case of mumps; discharged to duty 2; transferred to Lahore Casualty Clearing Station 1. GMT. | |
| 12.2.15. | A little snow last night, a cold dull day, some rain. Admitted 4; 2 discharged to duty; 1 transferred to C.C.S. GMT. | |
| 13.2.15. | Rain + wind with an occasional gleam of sunshine. Cold - Admitted 2, including one case of measles; discharged to duty 4; transferred to C.C.S. 3. GMT. | |
| 14.2.15. | Another bad day - gale of wind + incessant rain - admitted 6, including 1 case of measles; discharged to duty 4; transferred to C.C.S. 2. GMT. | |

Gulab Singh & Sons, Calcutta—No. 22 Army C.—5-8-14—1,07,000.

Army Form C. 2118.

# WAR DIARY
## INTELLIGENCE SUMMARY.
*(Erase heading not required.)*

63.

Instructions regarding War Diaries and Intelligence Summaries are contained in F. S. Regs., Part II, and the Staff Manual respectively. Title pages will be prepared in manuscript.

| Hour, Date, Place. | Summary of Events and Information. | Remarks and references to Appendices. |
|---|---|---|
| LA MIQUELLERIE 15. 2. 1915 | Weather Cold & wet. — Admitted 5, including one case of mumps; discharged to duty 1; Transferred to Casualty Clearing Station 3. | EMP |
| 16. 2. 1915 — | Frost last night, sun bright during day. Admitted 10, including one case of mumps; discharged to duty 1; Transferred to C.C.S. 5. | EMP |
| 17. 2. 1915 — | Snow and rain all day. Admitted 6, including one case of measles; discharged to duty 3; Transferred 5. | EMP |
| 18. 2. 1915 — | Raining all day. Admitted 8, including 1 case of measles, Transferred 8. | EMP |
| 19. 2. 1915 — | Quite fine today. Admitted 7, including 3 cases of mumps & 2 of measles; discharged to duty 2; Transferred 5. | EMP |
| 20. 2. 1915 — | Quite a nice fine day. Admitted 3, including one case of measles; discharged to duty 1; Transferred 1. | EMP |

Army Form C. 2118.

# WAR DIARY
## or
## INTELLIGENCE SUMMARY.
*(Erase heading not required.)*

Instructions regarding War Diaries and Intelligence Summaries are contained in F. S. Regs., Part II, and the Staff Manual respectively. Title pages will be prepared in manuscript.

64.

| Hour, Date, Place. | Summary of Events and Information. | Remarks and references to Appendices. |
|---|---|---|
| LA MIQUELLERIE 21.2.1915. | Fine day – Admitted 5, including 2 cases of mumps; discharged to duty 2; Transferred to Casualty Clearing Station Y. | discharged BMT |
| 22.2.1915. | Heavy fog last night, lover front this morning, fine to-day. Admitted 6, Transferred to C.C.S. 4. | BMT |
| 23.2.1915. | Foggy & cold, no rain – Admitted 8 including 1 case of mumps. Transferred 2. discharged to duty 1; | BMT |
| 24.2.1915. | Froze hard last night, snow & sleet to-day – Admitted 9, discharged to duty 1, transferred 2 – I have found it necessary in the course of this campaign to organise my field ambulance according to two new methods. After than the recognised trough organisation into four sections – A., B., C. & D. – and into two divisions, the Bearer division and the Tent division – The first of these new methods of organisation would I should think be useful or even necessary, at times in any campaign, either in India or in Europe, admitting that all four sections of the Field Ambulance keep together – This method of organisation | |

Gulab Singh & Sons, Calcutta—No. 22 Army C.—5-8-14—1,07,000.

**WAR DIARY**

*or*

**INTELLIGENCE SUMMARY.**

*(Erase heading not required.)*

Army Form C. 2118.

65 —

| Hour, Date, Place. | Summary of Events and Information. | Remarks and references to Appendices. |
|---|---|---|
| LA MIQUELERIE, 24.2.1915. | Arrived in the distribution of the whole of the personnel of the Field Ambulance in groups for the performance of certain duties by each group — e.g. a group for office work, a group for laundry work, a group but attached to kitchen, a group for washing the repair & completion of stores, clothing &c &c &c &c. The second our method of organisation, arriving in the distribution of the whole of the personnel and the whole of the equipment of the Field ambulance into ten sections. One which would be sent forward rapidly in case of need on a limited allowance of motor transport, viz. motor lorries & motor lorry transport, and the other which would follow up later with & on the ordinary horsed transport of the unit. GMc | |
| 25.2.1915 | More snow last night & this morning — fine today & sunny at times. Admitted 7, including 3 cases of Mumps, discharged to duty 6, transferred to C.C.S. 3. P.T.O. | |

Army Form C. 2118.

# WAR DIARY
## or
## INTELLIGENCE SUMMARY.
(Erase heading not required.)

66.

| Hour, Date, Place. | Summary of Events and Information. | Remarks and references to Appendices. |
|---|---|---|
| LA MIQUELLERIE 25.2.1915. | The following two British Officers have also been admitted today:- <br><br> 1. Major P. Sangster, 2nd Lancers, Brigade-Major Jodhpore Brigade. Since F.Y.D. (fever), transferred today to F.A.4 Casualty Clearing Station.- <br><br> 2. Lieut. H.V. Lewis, 129th Baluchis, Bomb wound right upper arm.- Lieut Lewis was engaged in bomb practice with his men when a bomb which had not been properly thrown by one of the men exploded and a shrapnel bullet from it lodged in Lieut. Lewis's arm just above the elbow. Three of his men were wounded by fragments of bomb at the same time, and they also have been admitted with my field ambulance.- EMM | |
| 26.2.1915. | Very frosty last night. Thaw today.- Sick, injured & enemy all day.- Admitted 8, including 4 cases of mumps, discharged to duty 4, transferred to Casualty Clearing Station Lieut Lewis and 9 men.- EMM | |

Gulab Singh & Sons, Calcutta—No. 22 Army C.—5-8-14—1,07,000.

# WAR DIARY

## INTELLIGENCE SUMMARY

Army Form C. 2118.

67.

(Erase heading not required.)

| Hour, Date, Place. | Summary of Events and Information. | Remarks and references to Appendices. |
|---|---|---|
| LA MIQUELLERIE 27.2.1915- | Sharp frost last night – Cloudy & cold today with strong wind and some snow – Admitted 12, including one case of mumps; discharged to duty 4; transferred 5. One case of Mumps transferred to Lahore Casualty Clearing Station 8. EMP | |
| 28.2.1915- | Fine bright sunny day – Admitted 20, including 8 cases of mumps; discharged to duty 4; transferred 5. The Indian troops followers have been very well fed and very well clothed, and have in my opinion stood the rigours of a winter campaign in the north of France very well indeed – Considering the exposure & hardships inseparable from such an experience there has been no undue prevalence of disease, and especially no undue prevalence of serious disease – EMFrost. Lt. Col. I.M.S. Com. of 92. III 9 F.A. Brigade & S.M.O. Ferozepore Brigade. | |

Serial No. 153

S 1st/31st March 1915    121/31114

**WAR DIARY**
**OF**
111 Indian Field Ambulance
From 1st March 1915 to 31st March 1915.

Confidential.

Army Form C. 2118.

# WAR DIARY

of Lieut Colonel H.H. Smart, I.M.S.,
Commanding N.III Indian Field Ambulance
and S.M.O., Ferozepore Brigade.

Intelligence

INTELLIGENCE SUMMARY.
(Erase heading not required.)

Vol. VII.

68.

Instructions regarding War Diaries and Intelligence Summaries are contained in F. S. Regs., Part II, and the Staff Manual respectively. Title pages will be prepared in manuscript.

| Hour, Date, Place. | Summary of Events and Information. From 1.3.1915 — to 31.3.1915 — | Remarks and references to Appendices. |
|---|---|---|
| LA MIQUELLERIE 1.3.1915. | Cloudy, windy, cold. Major A. Fenton, I.M.S. joined my field ambulance for duty to-day. Admitted 13; discharged to duty 1; transferred to Lahore Casualty Clearing Station 13. | A.M.W. O/C N.III.F.A. |
| 2.3.1915. | Cold, some wind. Bright & sunny during day. Admitted 17, including 1 case of mumps; discharged to duty 3; transferred 6. | A.M.W. |
| 3.3.1915. | Cloudy & dark, rain. Admitted 5, including 1 case of mumps; transferred 15. | A.M.W. |
| 4.3.1915. | Cloudy, no rain, not cold. Admitted 2, including 1 case of mumps; discharged to duty 3; transferred 7. | A.M.W. |

Army Form C. 2118.

# WAR DIARY
## or
## INTELLIGENCE SUMMARY.
(Erase heading not required.)

Instructions regarding War Diaries and Intelligence Summaries are contained in F. S. Regs., Part II, and the Staff Manual respectively. Title pages will be prepared in manuscript.

69.

| Hour, Date, Place. | Summary of Events and Information. | Remarks and references to Appendices. |
|---|---|---|
| LA MIQUELLERIE. 5.3.1915. | Cloudy, no rain, not cold. Admitted 7, discharged to duty 11, transferred 3. | GMT |
| 6.3.15. | Clouds & rain, not very cold. Admitted 3, including 2 cases of mumps, discharged to duty 1, transferred to Casualty Clearing Station 5. | GMT |
| 7.3.15. | Clouds, rain, wind. Cold. Admitted 68, including 3 cases of mumps, discharged to duty 2, transferred 7. The numerous admissions today are due to the fact that the Ferozepore Brigade is marching forward towards the trenches tonight, and men who have been detained under treatment in their regiments in the hope they can only return to duty have necessarily been sent into my field ambulance. | GMT |
| 8.3.15. | High wind from the north east, very cold. Have been orderly to clear my field ambulance, close and hold myself ready to move at short notice. Admitted none, discharged to duty 14, transferred to No.3 C.C.S. 60, remaining 3. S.A.S. Kishen Chand, 9.D.?, 9.11, 9.F.A. has been transferred sick from us to upper S.M.D. Ferozepore Brigade, as it has left this area. | GMT |

# WAR DIARY
## INTELLIGENCE SUMMARY.
*(Erase heading not required.)*

Army Form C. 2118.

70–

| Hour, Date, Place. | Summary of Events and Information. | Remarks and references to Appendices. |
|---|---|---|
| LA MIQUELLERIE 9.3.1915– | Sharp frost last night. Cold wind from the N.E. today. Snow this evening. One admitted, one discharged, remaining 3, eight cases. Ordered to move early tomorrow morning to LE CORNET MALO. | |
| LE CORNET MALO 10.3.15– | Marched here in the early morning. Remaining 3, eight cases. Some snow last night, followed by a sharp frost. Cloudy & cold today. Lieut. T.W.R. STRODE, R.A.M.C. (Temp.), joined for duty today. | |
| 11.3.15– | Cloudy & Cold. Lieut. out Ony bearer division today under command of Capt. D.C.V. Fitzgerald, I.M.S., to report to A.D.M.S., Meerut Division, at VIEILLE CHAPELLE for the purpose of helping to bring in wounded; and Lent the personnel of my tent division under command of Major A. Fenton, I.M.S., to report to the O.C. No D 1289.7.O. at ZELOBES for the purpose of helping him to treat wounded. Our attack on the Germans yesterday was very successful and we have seized & occupied Fesspre Chapelle and the German trenches east of it. | |

Army Form C. 2118.

# WAR DIARY
# — or —
# INTELLIGENCE SUMMARY.
(Erase heading not required.)

7.

| Hour, Date, Place. | Summary of Events and Information. | Remarks and references to Appendices. |
|---|---|---|
| LE CORNET MALO 12.3.15. | Fine day but foggy. The province of Spring is with us. Bearer Division is out at Vieille Chapelle & Richebourg with Capt. D.C.F. Fitzgerald I.M.S., and the personnel of the Bull Division at ZELOBES, depot at Le Cornet Malo. The Germans have lost very heavily in killed, wounded & prisoners, besides yielding ground to our troops. | BMP |
| 13.3.15. | Fine bright sunny day. Personnel of Bull Division returned today, forenoon, to Le Combt Malo, and the Bearer Division this evening. | BMP |
| 14.3.15. | Fine but hazy. We retain Neuve Chapelle and the ground immediately to the east of it. | BMP |
| 15.3.15. | Fine, but cloudy & hazy, not cold. All forms on Counter-attacks on Neuve Chapelle have been repulsed. The German losses inflicted in the recent fighting by the Indian Army Corps and the British 4th Corps, are estimated at 16,000 killed & wounded, and we have taken close on 2000 prisoners. It is the first heavy blow that the Indian Army Corps has administered to the enemy in nearly six months fighting. | BMP |

Army Form C. 2118.

# WAR DIARY
or
## INTELLIGENCE SUMMARY.
(Erase heading not required.)

72.

| Hour, Date, Place. | Summary of Events and Information. | Remarks and references to Appendices. |
|---|---|---|
| LE CORNET MALO 16.3.1915. | Fine Spring day but hazy. The Indian troops & followers are much happier now than they were during the rigours of the mid-winter months. They are also very cheery about the recent great successes at Neuve Chapelle, which they thoroughly understand was a severe blow to the Germans. It is the first time since they entered the firing line on the 22nd October 1914 that the Indian troops have had any chance of scoring a victory. Heretofore they have been always outnumbered by the enemy and hard put to it to hold their own. EMK. | |
| 17.3.15. | Fine bright sunny day. | |
| 18.3.15. | Fine day but foggy. Lt. A. Kennedy, I.M.S., returned from sick leave. Myself left on the 3/8 January and has been treated at the Base Hospital Boulogne and at Queen Mary's Convalescent Home for British Officers at Cimiez, Nice. EMK. | |
| 19.3.15. | Snow last night. Very cold today with a high wind tending towards. EMK. | |
| 20.3.15. | A little snow last night. Bright sunny today with a keen cold wind. EMK. | |
| 21.3.15. | Beautiful day — bright sunny & warm. EMK. | |

# WAR DIARY

## INTELLIGENCE SUMMARY

Army Form C. 2118.

73.

(Erase heading not required.)

| Hour, Date, Place. | Summary of Events and Information. | Remarks and references to Appendices. |
|---|---|---|
| LE CORNET MALO 22.3.15. | Frost last night. Bright & sunny & rather foggy. BMR | |
| 23.3.15. | Fine day - bright & sunny. | BMR |
| 24.3.15. | Mild, wet day. Lt Col Frost & Major A. Fenton departed on 7 days leave to the United Kingdom | W.H. Cary |
| Paradis 25.3.15 | A wet, cold day. Unit moved this morning to new billets at Paradis & occupied the billets viewed by No 129 9.B.F. Frost at night. Fine but cold day. | 6 H.C. |
| 26.3.15 | The F.A. was opened for reception of sick but no patients were received. | 6 H.C. |
| 27.3.15 | Hard frost at night. Day cold & generally fine but occasional snow showers. F.A. admitted 4 patients & temporarily & CCS. Capt Reinhold returned to Unit to forenoon after sick leave. | W.H.C. |

Army Form C. 2118.

74.

# WAR DIARY
## or
## INTELLIGENCE SUMMARY.

(Erase heading not required.)

Instructions regarding War Diaries and Intelligence Summaries are contained in F. S. Regs, Part II, and the Staff Manual respectively. Title pages will be prepared in manuscript.

| Hour, Date, Place. | Summary of Events and Information. | Remarks and references to Appendices. |
|---|---|---|
| Paradis 28/3/15 | Hard frost at night. Cold, bright day. Patients admitted 6, including 1 case of mumps; one patient trans? to C.C.S.8" | W.H.A. |
| 29/3/15 | Hard frost at night. Very cold but bright day. Patients admitted 6, including one case of mumps. Transferred to C.C.S. 4. | WHC |
| 30/3/15 | Hard frost at night. Cold bright day. Patients admitted 3; transferred to C.C.S.6 | WHC |
| PARADIS 31.3.15 to ZELOBES. | Fine bright breezy day — Cold. Lt. Col. L.H. Prosh, I.M.S., returned from 7 days' leave to England, and resumed command of the 9. Ambulance. Marched from Paradis to Zelobes where the 9. Cavy. Bde. received all Indian wounded & sick of the Lahore Division, which goes into the trenches today. Handed over billets at Paradis to No. 130 9.F.A. and to K men billets at Zelobes from No. 130 9.F.A. Admitted 8 wounded + 23 sick — Transferred 9 sick — | W.H.C.  L.H.Prosh, Lt.Col.I.M.S. Comdg.9 Ind.F.A. |

# WAR DIARY

## OF

No. 111 Indian Field Ambulance.

From 1st April 1915 to 30 April 1915

**Confidential**

# WAR DIARY

of Lieut. Colonel G.H.Y. Knott, I.M.S.
(Comdg. 9. Indian Field Ambulance)
Comdg. 9. Indian Field Ambulance

## INTELLIGENCE SUMMARY.

Vol. VIII

(Erase heading not required.)

Army Form C. 2118.

Instructions regarding War Diaries and Intelligence Summaries are contained in F. S. Regs., Part II, and the Staff Manual respectively. Title pages will be prepared in manuscript.

From 1.4.1915 to 30.4.1915.

| Hour, Date, Place. | Summary of Events and Information. | Remarks and references to Appendices. |
|---|---|---|
| ZELOBES. 1.4.1915. | Finest day but Cold. Admitted 15 sick, including 4 cases of mumps: and 5 wounded. Transferred to Casualty Clearing Station 18 sick and 7 wounded. | GHYKnott Lt. Col. I.M.S. Comdg 9 Ind F.A. |
| 2.4.15. | Fine day but Cold - a good deal of rain last night. Admitted 28 sick, including 9 cases of mumps; and 5 wounded, including one wound of left hand. Transferred to C.C.S. 25 sick and 5 wounded. | GHYK |
| 3.4.15. | Cold & wet. Admitted 20 sick, including 5 cases of mumps; and 7 wounded, including one wound of right hand. Transferred to C.C.S. 22 sick & 5 wounded. Discharged to duty 1 sick man recovered. Since the 31.3.15 my field ambulance has been augmented, taking in all the wounded & sick Indians of the whole of the Lahore Division. | GHYK |

# WAR DIARY
## INTELLIGENCE SUMMARY.
*(Erase heading not required.)*

Army Form C. 2118.

| Hour, Date, Place. | Summary of Events and Information. | Remarks and references to Appendices. |
|---|---|---|
| ZELOBES. 4.4.1915. | Cold & wet. Admitted 43 sick, including 12 cases of mumps, and 17 wounded, including one wound of left hand. Transferred to Casualty Clearing Station 2 sick & 7 wounded. One wounded man, shot in the town, died in the F.A. | AMR |
| 5.4.15. | Cold & wet. Admitted 8 sick, including 4 cases of mumps, and 7 wounded, including 1 wound of right hand. Transferred to C.C.S. 3 sick and 16 wounded. | AMR |
| 6.4.15. | Cold & wet, with a strong wind. Admitted 39 sick, including 4 cases of mumps, and 17 wounded - no hand wounds - Transferred to C.C.S. 27 sick & 7 wounded. Discharged to duty 2 cases recovered. | AMR |

Army Form C. 2118.

# WAR DIARY
## or
## INTELLIGENCE SUMMARY.
(Erase heading not required.)

Instructions regarding War Diaries and Intelligence Summaries are contained in F. S. Regs., Part II, and the Staff Manual respectively. Title pages will be prepared in manuscript.

| Hour, Date, Place. | Summary of Events and Information. | Remarks and references to Appendices. |
|---|---|---|
| ZELOBES. 7.4.1915. | Hard cold rain showers with a strong wind. Admitted sick:- 1 Officer (British) and 43 Indian ranks including 9 cases of mumps - wounded 11, including 1 case of wound of left hand. All these cases have been marked "not suspicious" by the A.D.M.S. Lahore Division. I mentioned a case of wound of left hand, blackened at 1 Murphy by powder (it was a slight graze of the ulnar border of the left hand, blackened at 1 Murphy by powder) of British officer. Transferring to Casualty Clearing Station on British Officer, with mumps, and 46 Indian ranks, also 10 wounded - Discharged to duty 3 sick, recovered. | [signature] |
| 8.4.15. | Blowing a gale with hard cold showers of rain. Admitted 83 sick, including 7 cases of mumps, 2 of measles, and 1 first of trenchfoot in two ten feet Clinente, due to exposure to cold + wet - 1 not in the trenches, and 18 wounded, including 6 head cases, 3 right & 3 left. All these | [signature] |

**WAR DIARY**
or
**INTELLIGENCE SUMMARY.**
(Erase heading not required.)

Army Form C. 2118.

72.

| Hour, Date, Place. | Summary of Events and Information. | Remarks and references to Appendices. |
|---|---|---|
| ZELOBES. 8.4.1915. | Six hand cases have been marked as "not suspicious" both by me and by the A.D.M.S., Lahore Division. The left hand wound which I marked as "suspicious" yesterday the 7.4.15, was also thought to be suspicious by Major A. Denton, D.M.S. and Major W.H. Caffary, D.M.S., but the A.D.M.S. considered it "not suspicious." Transferred to Casualty Clearing Station 33 sick and 19 wounded. Discharged to duty 2 sick, recovered. | SMP |
| 9.4.15. | Very Cold. Kept wind from the West veering to the North. Had sleet & hail and very cold raw showers. Admitted 34 sick including 2 enemy rumph, 1 measles and 7 foot cases, chronic; also 22 wounded including 1 left hand & right hand wounds. All these six hand wounds have been marked "not suspicious" both by me and by the A.D.M.S. Lahore Division. Transferred to C.C.S. 34 sick & 14 wounded. Discharged to duty 1 sick, recovered. | SMP |

# WAR DIARY
## INTELLIGENCE SUMMARY.
*(Erase heading not required.)*

Army Form C. 2118.

73.

Instructions regarding War Diaries and Intelligence Summaries are contained in F. S. Regs., Part II, and the Staff Manual respectively. Title pages will be prepared in manuscript.

| Hour, Date, Place. | Summary of Events and Information. | Remarks and references to Appendices. |
|---|---|---|
| ZELOBES. 10.4.1915 | Cold hard dry wind from the north west — no rain. Admitted 53 sick, including five cases of mumps, and 20 cases of swollen feet and exposure, due to exposure to cold & wet in the trenches; also wounded 1 British (Officer) + 19 Indian ranks - no hand wounds. Transferred to C.C.S. 5 — 2 sick, and 1 British Officer + 23 Indian ranks wounded. Two wounded men (1 head + 1 chest) died in the R.A. | JMcM |
| 11.4.15. | Cold hard dry wind. Admitted 37 sick, including 1 case of mumps + 13 swollen feet, climatic; also wounded 14, including 6 hand cases, 1 right + 5 left. Of these two wounds of the left hand were markedly "suspicious" Both by me and by the A.D.M.S., Lahore Division. These two cases were also seen and considered suspicious by the D.D.M.S., Indian Army Corps. (Colonel Pike R.A.M.C.) | |

# WAR DIARY

## INTELLIGENCE SUMMARY

Army Form C. 2118.

74.

| Hour, Date, Place. | Summary of Events and Information. | Remarks and references to Appendices. |
|---|---|---|
| ZELOBES 11.4.15 | and by Majors A. Fenton I.M.S. & W.H. Cazaly I.M.S. and by Capt. C.H. Reinhold I.M.S. Transferred to C.C.S. 35 sick & 15 wounded. Discharged to duty 1 wounded & 1 sick, recovered. | JMS |
| 12.4.15. | Cold & dry. Admitted 41 sick, including 2 cases of mumps & 14 sunstroke feet climate; also 9 wounded. Transferred to C.C.S. 40 sick and 13 wounded. Discharged to duty 1 wounded and 8 sick, recovered. | JMS |
| 13.4.15. | Fine, cloudy, cold. Admitted 13 sick, including 4 cases of mumps; no wounded. Transferred to C.C.S. 13 sick & 8 wounded. Transferred to N.º 118 I.F.A. 6 cases of Scabies, english cases of left hand wounds, marked suspicious. Handed over to 12/130 I.F.A. billets at ZELOBES. Relieved to ROBECQ and to K.B.R. billets near CALONNE. N.º 128 I.F.A. The Lahore Division has been relieved by the Meerut Division. Out of the trenches today and been replaced by the Meerut Division. | JMS |

Army Form C. 2118.

# WAR DIARY
## or
## INTELLIGENCE SUMMARY.
(Erase heading not required.)

75-

| Hour, Date, Place. | Summary of Events and Information. | Remarks and references to Appendices. |
|---|---|---|
| ROBECQ. 14.4.15. | For the day, wind, cold. Some rain - 2 inst & evening in afternoon - | BMF - |
| 15.4.15. | Bright, sunny day - coldish - occupied in cleaning up, refitting, rifling, training + instructing &c - Major H Hopwell proceeded to different units - in seven days leave - | BMF - |
| 16.4.15. | Very fine day, bright + drying - | BMF - |
| 17.4.15. | Very fine day - bright + sunny but cold - | BMF - |
| 18.4.15. | Beautiful day - bright + sunny - | BMF - |
| 19.4.15. | Perfect day - bright sunny all day - cloudless sky - decent [illegible] has occurred in the number of a Hospital Orderlies casualty - Lieut. A. Kennedy proceeded to England on 7 days leave - | BMF - |
| 20.4.15. | Fine day cold - east wind - Two Army Reserve Leave developed Mumps today - | BMF - |
| 21.4.15. | Very fine weather, but cold - N.B. wind - | BMF - |

**Army Form C. 2118.**

# WAR DIARY
## or
## INTELLIGENCE SUMMARY.
*(Erase heading not required.)*

Instructions regarding War Diaries and Intelligence Summaries are contained in F. S. Regs., Part II, and the Staff Manual respectively. Title pages will be prepared in manuscript.

| Hour, Date, Place. | Summary of Events and Information. | Remarks and references to Appendices. |
|---|---|---|
| ROBECQ — 22.4.1915 | Very fine day — bright & sunny — Intd O.R with N.S. Irving — but Col R with N.S. Irving returned from 7 days leave in England, and was at once summoned to the headquarters of the Lahore Division to take charge of the Sanitary Section of the Meerut Division to take charge of the Lahore Division. Three cases of Mumps were transferred to No 3 F.A. | Major W.H. Cagely |
| 23.4.15 | a fine bright sunny weather. Air very cool with a sharp biting wind from the East. Received orders to be ready to move. Any field ambulances of Brigade at church where Lieut. J.F. Anderson, I.M.S., rejoined No. 111 F.F.A. F.day. | bring wind from the East. |
| ROBECQ to MONT DESCATS. 24.4.15 | Marched today from Robecq to Mont Descats, near the Belgian Border. Distance about 20 miles; time 3.30 p.m. to 2 a.m. — Very cold, hard biting wind from the north east — Much dust on the march, later some very cold rain at 1 a.m. | |
| MONT DESCATS to OUDERDOM 25.4.15 | Marched to-day from Mont Descats to Ouderdom, crossing into Belgium near Westoutre. Distance about 12 miles; time 9 a.m. to 4.30 p.m. Received orders to March back to Mont Descats tomorrow morning. | |

Army Form C. 2118.

# WAR DIARY
## or
## INTELLIGENCE SUMMARY.

(Erase heading not required.)

| Hour, Date, Place. | Summary of Events and Information. | Remarks and references to Appendices. |
|---|---|---|
| OUDERDOM to MONT DESCATS 26.4.1915 | Marched back from Ouderdom to Mont Descats today. Established my field ambulance in the monastery of the Trappist Monks. This is already occupied by the Casualty Clearing Station of the 28th Division under the command of Lt. Col. W.F. Poole, R.A.M.C. (T.) who promises to make room for sick & wounded Indians and to give me all the aid he can as he is with Ind[?] I have been detailed to perform with my field ambulance the duty of a Casualty Clearing Station for Indians, & from what I see during the progress of the battle now raging in the Lahore Division, (working hereabouts by regiments from the type of tent Chapiels to the rear of Ypres there will be doubtless lots of heavy work ahead. Took over from 10 & 15. F.A. 115 sick Indians — Relieved Capt. A.J. Anderson with necessary personnel to medical & press on sections. Lent. J.P. Anderson with necessary personnel & medicines to press on infections diseases hospital at Ondewardsyvelde near Railway Station. BMP | 7 a.m. to 12 noon. |
| MONT DESCATS 27.4.1915 | Very fine day, but heavy & cold. Long convoy of sick Indians yesterday the Lahore Division became heavily engaged in the afternoon. Received during last night 115 wounded Indians. Despatched this afternoon by ambulance train 40 to[?] Oudenardsvelde 116 wounded Indians. | BMP |

# WAR DIARY or INTELLIGENCE SUMMARY

Army Form C. 2118.

| Hour, Date, Place. | Summary of Events and Information. | Remarks and references to Appendices. |
|---|---|---|
| MONT DESCATS. 28.4.1915. | Fine day but thick haze & strong wind - quieted - Received last night 17 wounded Indian officers and 923 rank & file; also 63 Indian sick & skull & hit; also 1 wounded French Moroccan Soldier and 4 wounded French Moroccan Soldiers - These were cleared today by Motor Ambulances to St Omer, Hazebrouck, Blaris & St Omer - Surg. Rebrand Porter, D.M.S., 2nd Army, came and inspected and made arrangements here on the 26th & 27th Inst - | |
| 29.4.15 | Beautiful day, bright & sunny - Received 7 wounded Indian Officers and 219 rank & file - also 2 & sick Indians - Lieut. A. Kennedy, who was detached yesterday with one section to Hazebrouck, reported today - Field Marshal Sir John French inspected my field Ambulance Clearing Station today and said that Col. Peake & I had done Splendidly and that everything was most satisfactory - He went through all the wards and personally spoke to every wounded Soldier, British & Indian, Speaking to many of them - Surg. General O'Donnell, D.M.S., Indl Army, also visited [illegible] today and was quite satisfied that everything was all right - DMS | |

# WAR DIARY
## INTELLIGENCE SUMMARY

*(Erase heading not required.)*

Army Form C. 2118.

| Hour, Date, Place. | Summary of Events and Information | Remarks and references to Appendices. |
|---|---|---|
| MONT DESCATS - 30.4.15 | Beautiful day, very bright & sunny & quiet - but - Received 44 wounded Indians and 10 died - Transferred wounded & sick by motor ambulances towards the base - [signature] Lt Col. I.M.S. Comdg offr 111 I.F.A. | |

Serial No. 153.

121/5799

# WAR DIARY
## OF

No. 111 ~~Brit~~ Indian Field Ambulance. – Lahore Division

From 1 May 1915 to 31st May 1915.

May 1915

**Army Form C. 2118**

**Confidential**

Instructions regarding War Diaries and Intelligence Summaries are contained in F. S. Regs., Part II, and the Staff Manual respectively. Title pages will be prepared in manuscript.

# WAR DIARY
## or
## INTELLIGENCE SUMMARY.
*(Erase heading not required.)*

Unit: Officer Comdg. 145th (N.S.) Coy of Willesden Field Ambulance

From 1.5.1915 to 31.5.1915

Vol 2

[Stamp: A.B.S. OFFICE AT THE BASE — 7 JUN 1915 — INDIAN SECTION]

| Hour, Date, Place. | Summary of Events and Information | Remarks and references to Appendices. |
|---|---|---|
| MONT DESCATS. 1.5.1915 | Beautiful day; bright sunny, quite warm. Received 46 sick & 56 wounded, including one Indian officer. | [initials] |
| 2.5.15 | Cloudy but fine, no rain — very cold with N.E. wind. Received 53 sick & 29 wounded. Returned to duty 10 sick, then reported to the Calais Division. Received 8 wounded, including one Indian officer. | [initials] |
| 3.5.15 | Beautiful day — Fine, bright, sunny, but very cold with N.E. wind. Received 8 wounded & 18 sick. | [initials] |
| 4.5.15 | Charming day; fine, bright, sunny — mild. Some rain last night. Received 29 sick. Several cases of pneumonia & chlorine poisoning. Gas have been received during the last few days, but the acute stage had passed away by the time they arrived in my Field Ambulance. | [initials] |

Army Form C. 2118.

81.

# WAR DIARY
## or
## INTELLIGENCE SUMMARY.
(Erase heading not required.)

| Hour, Date, Place. | Summary of Events and Information | Remarks and references to Appendices. |
|---|---|---|
| MONT DESCATS. 5.5.1915 | Bright & fine with a thick haze. Quite warm. A delightful spring day. Some rain last night none today. Evacuated all remaining wounded and sick to Clearing Stations. | RMM |
| " 6.5.15. | Beautiful day. Bright, sunny & warm. Nightingales & blackbirds singing all round. Lieut. F.J. Anderson, I.M.S., having satisfactorily closed his Inflation Disease Hospital at Godeswaervelde, rejoined my headquarters. Marched at 8 p.m. for L'Epinette. Had a very friendly send off from A. Col. W.P. Peake R.A.M.C.(T) and the Officers (R.A.M.C.(T) both Reg[ula]r & [Ter]r[i]tor[ia]l of the North Midland Division Clearing Station, who had received us and treated us most kindly & hospitably during our stay at Mont Descats. | RMM |
| L'EPINETTE. 7.5.15. | Arrived and went into billets at 3 a.m. Bright day. Allowed all my personnel to have a rest today as far as possible. Sent 80 sick, including two prisoners with wounds (slight) prisoner Number. Sie. Self-inflicted by means of their own rifles to No. 1/3 N.M.F.A. Discharged to duty with their regiments — | RMM |
| " 8.5.15. | Beautiful day; fine, bright & sunny. Published orders clearly having Troops to establish and ensure sanitary conditions in billets — held a Cond[uc]t[ing] [Recon?] of British front to No 6 [?] and observe munitions movement. [?] which have [?] admittedly and inform demsends [?] | RMM |

Army Form C. 2118.

82 -

# WAR DIARY
## INTELLIGENCE SUMMARY.
*(Erase heading not required.)*

| Hour, Date, Place. | Summary of Events and Information | Remarks and references to Appendices. |
|---|---|---|
| L'ÉPINETTE, 9.5.15. | Beautiful, bright, sunny day. (Whit-Sunday) Heavy attack upon the Germans today by our 1st Army, partly for the purpose of aiding the French who are attacking their heavy trench south of the La Bassée Canal — a very artillery bombardment was carried out from 5 a.m. to 8 a.m., our troops from 3.30 a.m. to 5 a.m. Infantry attacks moved off somewhere about 5 by the 1st Army front from the La Bassée Canal to Laventie. Our trenches were captured by us near Fromelles. Mr. P. Aushelaure's kidneys trouble — Major A. Fenton, R.M.S., has been appointed cheerless in advanced Operating Surgery to my D.A. | The previous today |
| 10.5.15. | Beautiful day, sunny & bright, and quite left in the sun — went out to the trenches near Fleur Chapelle & learn the medical arrangements there. | SMF |
| 11.5.15. | Charming day, sunny, bright & warm with Orvil carrying. Had all British & Indian personnel examined to see that they are properly identity discs, trousers, hay-boots, first field dressings iron rations add serviceable & well-fitting boots and that men feet are in good condition. | SMF |

Gulab Singh & Sons, Calcutta—No. 22 Army C—5-8-14—1,07,000.

# WAR DIARY
## INTELLIGENCE SUMMARY.

*(Erase heading not required.)*

Army Form C. 2118.

83

| Hour, Date, Place. | Summary of Events and Information | Remarks and references to Appendices. |
|---|---|---|
| L'EPINETTE. 12.5.15. | Perfect day – bright, sunny, breeze – wind has reached high. Had an inspection of all personnel British & Indian, for inoculator against small-pox and inoculation against enteric fever. Those requiring protection in these respects will now be protected – all present with the F.A. were inoculated – both British & Indian recruits against enteric fever in January. In April twelve men (British & Indian) who had fever since January were inoculated. Similarly all newly British & Indian – who required protection against small-pox – were inoculated in April. EMM | |
| " 13.5.15. | Cloudy & cool – nice soft gentle rain last night & today – Lieut. A. Kennedy, I.M.S. was transferred today to the 4g.E. Cavalries. and Temp: Lieut. M.L. Bhandari, I.M.S. reported himself up to do duty. The clothing of all Indian personnel was inspected today, to see that it was all bright and to reduce to minimum scale. EMM | |
| " 14.5.15. | Cloudy – windy – cool. Turned very cold indeed at night & left and pm. Have published an order warning all ranks against the danger of frost-bite & against the necessity of precautions especially in trenches, clothes in which by men are collected. EMM | |

Gulab Singh & Sons, Calcutta—No. 22 Army C.—5-8-14—1,07,000.

/ Army Form C. 2118.

84 -

# WAR DIARY
## INTELLIGENCE SUMMARY.
(Erase heading not required.)

| Hour, Date, Place. | Summary of Events and Information | Remarks and references to Appendices. |
|---|---|---|
| L'EPINETTE. 15.5.1915. | Sharp frost last night. — Beautiful weather today. — Bright, sunny, warm. The field ambulance is under orders to be ready to march at any short notice. — | |
| " 16.5.15. | Lovely day. — Sunny, bright & warm. — The F. Ambulance is held ready to march immediately on receipt of orders. — | Heavy fighting here, our troops attacking. |
| " 17.5.15. | Rain last night & today. — Our troops have been winning German trenches and capturing German prisoners. — The F. Ambulance is still under orders to be ready to march at a moment's notice. — Orders have been issued for work to be careful of all glass syringes as the available supply of these is running short. — | |
| " 18.5.15. | Steady strong rain last night. — Cold. N.E. wind. Took my leave driver to St. VAAST and left it there under the command of Capt. J.T. ANDERSON to assist in the work of the advanced Dressing Station of the MEERUT Division. — | |
| " 19.5.15. | Quite cold. — N.E. wind and slight rain. — Shall day at the advanced dressing station at St. VAAST and at the trenches along the Rue du Bois. — Special arrangements are now being made for the distribution of flies, manure and food refuse. — | |

Army Form C. 2118.

85.

# WAR DIARY
## or
## INTELLIGENCE SUMMARY.
(Erase heading not required.)

Instructions regarding War Diaries and Intelligence Summaries are contained in F. S. Regs., Part II, and the Staff Manual respectively. Title pages will be prepared in manuscript.

| Hour, Date, Place. | Summary of Events and Information | Remarks and references to Appendices. |
|---|---|---|
| L'EPINETTE. 20.5.15. | Fine day, sunny & bright. My Reserve Division returned from St: VAAST today. | GMT |
| 21.5.15 | Steady soft summer rain. Very severe cannonade tonight. Our troops are attacking tonight. As the farm in which I was very small & cramped I have moved my Headquarters to an empty farm 600 yards to the South nearer LA CROIX MARMUSE in which the accommodation available for myself is much better. | This everiut- _____ P. Epinette was _____ the enemy LA CROIX MARMUSE — GMT. |
| La CROIX MARMUSE. 22.5.15. | Fine warm bright day. Heavy Cannonade in the evening to the South, apparently beyond the La Bassée canal, where the left of the French. Issued detailed orders upon the measures to be carried out for the destruction of flies, manure and food refuse &c. | GMT. |
| 23.5.15. | Beautiful day — sunny, bright and quiet day. Each word - notified the introduction of the field medical card with instructions _____ in place of Tally. Also warned all M.Os & Dressers of the danger of applying bandages too tightly to wounded limbs. Moved my field ambulance back to P. Epinette this afternoon. | GMT. |

Gulab Singh & Sons, Calcutta—No. 22 Army C.—5-8-14—1,07,000.

# WAR DIARY

## or INTELLIGENCE SUMMARY.

(Erase heading not required.)

Army Form C. 2118.

86.

Instructions regarding War Diaries and Intelligence Summaries are contained in F. S. Regs., Part II, and the Staff Manual respectively. Title pages will be prepared in manuscript.

| Hour, Date, Place. | Summary of Events and Information | Remarks and references to Appendices. |
|---|---|---|
| L'EPINETTE, 24.5.15. | Bright sunny summer day. Cloudless sky – quiet day – exchanged heavy cannonade & musketry for half night. Returned in morning. Found it necessary to arrange by an order in detail for the strict distribution of the full authorized amount of fuel & all rations. British & Indian, in fair estd. | MMT |
| " 25.5.15. | Cloudless sky, hot summer day. Received orders at 11 AM. to march to Calonne – Sur – La – Lys, and billet there. During morning fatigue parties were employed in covering in & making middens with earth and levelling ground in horse lines by spade work and rolling. Making great reductions in the piles of young corn. | MMT |
| CALONNE 26.5.15. | Cloudless sky, hot summer day, cool wind. Busy in settling in, clearing ground &c. | MMT |
| " 27.5.15. | Cloudy & cool, northerly wind. Aeroplanes flying in shift. In a very strong wind. Gave a lecture & instruction in map reading to Teachy. Lieut. M.G. Bhandari, I.M.S. | MMT |

Army Form C. 2118.

87.

# WAR DIARY
## or
## INTELLIGENCE SUMMARY.
*(Erase heading not required.)*

| Hour, Date, Place. | Summary of Events and Information | Remarks and references to Appendices. |
|---|---|---|
| CALONNE. 28.5.15. | Cloudy & Cold – dry – Strong Keen wind from the north – Appointed No. 17093 Driv: J. Spencer, A.S.C. an unpaid Lance-Corporal in the full ambulance with effect from today. Had to punish two A.S.C. drivers Mayor & Leary, & Larelli without permission. Also an Army Bearer for having a lighted candle in billet contrary to orders. Final of wrestling competition this evening – winner of first prize; Army Bearer Munkiral, quite a cheery little wrestler and a very fast one at his weight; second prize to Gohar Ali. Also a good sturdy performer – An excellent match, decided by the winner of two throws out of three – All ranks much interested in the contest. GMT | |
| 29.5.15. | Cold, dry, Clear – north wind – Had to punish four A.S.C. drivers for drunkenness and disorderly conduct – midday when the sun was brightly shining Baptiste Lenard at | GMT |

Army Form C. 2118.

# WAR DIARY
## or
## INTELLIGENCE SUMMARY.

(Erase heading not required.)

Instructions regarding War Diaries and Intelligence Summaries are contained in F. S. Regs., Part II, and the Staff Manual respectively. Title pages will be prepared in manuscript.

88.

| Hour, Date, Place. | Summary of Events and Information | Remarks and references to Appendices. |
|---|---|---|
| CALONNE, 30.5.15. | Cloudy, Cold, dry – north wind – Fatigue parties at work as Cleaning & levelling ground in horse lines, and in covering our form middens with earth. | JMcI |
| " 31.5.15. | Sunny & bright, Cold – north wind – Received respirators for use against poisonous German gas – viz: 143 respirators for distribution among my personnel – It is now ordered than no straw will be allowed for bedding in trenches after this date; also sump which throughout the Winter was issued daily to men in the trenches and three weekly to all the troops at the front is to be stopped and will only be issued after today under special circumstances by the defender – | JMcI |

JMcIntosh. Lt. Col. I.M.S.
Com. 9.9 2 III 9.4.9.

Serial No. 153.

121/6/28

# WAR DIARY
## OF

No 111 Indian Field Ambulance. — Lahore Div.

From 1st June 1915. To 30th June 1915.

Army Form C. 2118.

Confidential

Instructions regarding War Diaries and Intelligence Summaries are contained in F. S. Regs., Part II, and the Staff Manual respectively. Title pages will be prepared in manuscript.

# WAR DIARY

*of* Lieut. Colonel E. H. Frost, M.S.
Comm'dg: No. 111. Indian Field Ambulance

## INTELLIGENCE SUMMARY.

VOL X

(Erase heading not required.)

From 1.6.1915 to 30.6.15

[Stamp: A.G.'s OFFICE AT THE BASE, No. 145 W.D., 3 JUL 1915, INDIAN SECTION]

89.

| Hour, Date, Place. | Summary of Events and Information. | Remarks and references to Appendices. |
|---|---|---|
| CALONNE 1.6.15 | Very fine day — bright sunny — D/Lieut. P. J. Walsh, I.M.S., reported his arrival last evening and is posted to the Command of D Section. Temp. Capt. M. G. BHANDARI, I.M.S., detailed on 31.5.15 evening for Boulogne, reported himself to O.C. Meerut Stationary Hospital for duty. Temp. Lieut. Bhandari had only seen a few days work with my field ambulance when he came to me and said he was quite unable to perform the duty of an officer with a field ambulance on service. Physically unfit to do it, and incapable of enduring what he called the "miserable conditions of life" — | E M Knapp Col RAMC IMS Comdg No III I.F.A. |

Army Form C. 2118.

90

# WAR DIARY
## or
## INTELLIGENCE SUMMARY.

(Erase heading not required.)

Instructions regarding War Diaries and Intelligence Summaries are contained in F. S. Regs., Part II, and the Staff Manual respectively. Title pages will be prepared in manuscript.

| Hour, Date, Place. | Summary of Events and Information. | Remarks and references to Appendices. |
|---|---|---|
| CALONNE 2.6.15 | Fine warm day; wind still Northerly. Lieut. P.J. Walsh I.M.S. reported his departure yesterday evening for duty with the M[eerut] Division. Lieut Colonel G.H. Frost I.M.S. was placed on the sick list today. Major A. Fenton I.M.S. assumed command of the Field Ambulance. | |
| 3-6-15 | Lieut Colonel G.H. Frost I.M.S. was invalided to no 2 (London) Casualty clearing station Merville, suffering from pleurisy (right). Day warm and generally fine; a few drops of rain fell in the afternoon. | 67. |
| 4-6-15 | Day fine generally; slight rain in forenoon; wind westerly. | 68. |

Gulab Singh & Sons, Calcutta—No. 22 Army C—5-8-14—1,07,000.

Army Form C. 2118.

# WAR DIARY
## or
## INTELLIGENCE SUMMARY.

(Erase heading not required.)

| Hour, Date, Place. | Summary of Events and Information. | Remarks and references to Appendices. |
|---|---|---|
| CALONNE 5-6-15 | Day fine; warm; with westerly wind. | |
| " 6-6-15 | Lieut A H Brown I.M.S. reported his arrival for duty at 8 P.M. from Secunderabad general hospital at Hardelot | L/B |
| " 7-6-15 | Very warm, sunny day; wind still westerly. | L/B |
| " 8-6-15 | Day oppressively hot. Thunderstorm with heavy rain in afternoon. Drew Fr 400/- (four hundred) on account of imprest for supplies from the field cashier. | L/B  A/B |
| " 9-6-15 | I handed over to Major H.M.H. Melhuish I.M.S. this afternoon | |

MAJOR. KM.H. MELHUISH. I.M.S. took over command from MAJOR. A. FENTON. I.M.S.

A. Fenton
Major I.M.S.

Army Form C. 2118.

# WAR DIARY
or
INTELLIGENCE SUMMARY.

92.

(Erase heading not required.)

Instructions regarding War Diaries and Intelligence Summaries are contained in F. S. Regs., Part II, and the Staff Manual respectively. Title pages will be prepared in manuscript.

| Hour, Date, Place. | Summary of Events and Information. | Remarks and references to Appendices. |
|---|---|---|
| CALONNE. 10-6-15. | Orders in relation from Lt.Col. A.D. Innes LAHORE DIVISION. CAPT. J.F. ANDERSON I.M.S. proceeded to temporary reserve charge of the 34th PIONEERS. Dull & overcast. Some rain & hail. | Sh. |
| 11-6-15. | Routini. Weather dull. Some showers. | Sh. |
| 12-6-15. | Three Motor Ambulances arrived from H.Q. Quarters to be temporarily attached to this unit. | Sh. |

Army Form C. 2118.

# WAR DIARY
## or
## INTELLIGENCE SUMMARY.

G3.

(Erase heading not required.)

Instructions regarding War Diaries and Intelligence Summaries are contained in F. S. Regs., Part II, and the Staff Manual respectively. Title pages will be prepared in manuscript.

| Hour, Date, Place. | Summary of Events and Information. | Remarks and references to Appendices. |
|---|---|---|
| CALONNE. | | |
| 13-6-15. | Routine. | |
| 14-6-15. | Lieut. J.G. JOHN I.M.S. joined from leave for temporary duty with this ambulance. | Mn. |
| 15-6-15. | LIEUT C.H.BAKER reported his departure to take charge of the 57th Rifles. Routine. Fine wind N.E. | Mn. |
| 16-6-15. | CAPT. C.H. REINHOLD I.M.S. reported departure for temporary duty with No 112 I.F. A. Routine. Weather. Got rain | Mn. |
| 17-6-15. | Routine. | Mn. |
| 18-6-15. | Do. | Mn. |
| 19-6-15. | Do. | Mn. |
| 20-6-15. | Do. weather do | Mn. |
| 21-6-15. | Do. do | Mn. |

Army Form C. 2118.

# WAR DIARY
## or
## INTELLIGENCE SUMMARY.

94.

(Erase heading not required.)

Instructions regarding War Diaries and Intelligence Summaries are contained in F. S. Regs., Part II, and the Staff Manual respectively. Title pages will be prepared in manuscript.

| Hour, Date, Place. | Summary of Events and Information. | Remarks and references to Appendices. |
|---|---|---|
| CALONNE. | | |
| 22-6-15. | Routine. | |
| 23-6-15. | do. | |
| 24-6-15. | LIEUT. H. H. BROWN IMS reported his departure for temporary medical charge of the 1/1st Gurkha Rifles. CAPT. D.C.V. FITZGERALD IMS reported his arrival for duty with detailed Ambulances. Mule airfield - true reserve cash. Weather. | |
| 25.6.15. | CAPT. C. H. REINHOLD IMS reported his return from temporary duty with 112 IFA. (Heavy rain) weather - rain. | |
| 26.6.15. | Routine. weather fair. Generally heavy thunderstorm. | |
| 27.6.15. | do. | |
| 28.6.15. | Routine. Early scouts march to Bazar log. | |

Army Form C. 2118.

# WAR DIARY

or

## INTELLIGENCE SUMMARY.   915.

*(Erase heading not required.)*

Instructions regarding War Diaries and Intelligence Summaries are contained in F. S. Regs., Part II, and the Staff Manual respectively. Title pages will be prepared in manuscript.

| Hour, Date, Place. | Summary of Events and Information. | Remarks and references to Appendices. |
|---|---|---|
| CALONNE. 29.6.15. | Lt. J.C. JOHN IMS reported to Headquarters temporary duty with No 113 JFA. Heathen. Showing | sd. |
| 30.6.15. | Routine. | sd. |
| | S. Mahmud Major & MC Comm'dg. 111 J.F.A | |

Serial No 153

121/6502

# WAR DIARY
## OF
111 Indian Field Ambulance

From 1st July 1915 To 31st July 1915.

July '15

**Army Form C. 2118.**

# WAR DIARY

## No 111 of AFA
## INTELLIGENCE SUMMARY.
## Vol XI

(Erase heading not required.)

Instructions regarding War Diaries and Intelligence Summaries are contained in F. S. Regs., Part II, and the Staff Manual respectively. Title pages will be prepared in manuscript.

96

| Hour, Date, Place. | Summary of Events and Information. | Remarks and references to Appendices. |
|---|---|---|
| CALONNE | | |
| 1-7-15. | The field Ambulances has unclosed duties. Routine parade. | RM. |
| 2-7-15. | No 1105 Pte Clarey Sub-Asst Surgeon KARTAR RAM reported to departure for duty with 21st Cavy Sappers & Miners. No 379 Sub Asst Surgeon GANPAT RAMJI R.A.M.C. reported his arrival for duty with the unit. | JM. |
| 3-7-15. | Weather exceptionally hot. Mosquitos chiefs Culex have made their appearance in large numbers. | JM. |
| 4-7-15 | Another day of exceptional heat. | RM. |
| 5-7-15. | Routine | RM. |
| 6-7-15 | Routine. | RM. |
| 7-7-15 | Routine. Stormy weather. Strong S.W. wind. Some rain. | RM. |

Army Form C. 2118.

# WAR DIARY
## or
## INTELLIGENCE SUMMARY.

97.

(Erase heading not required.)

Instructions regarding War Diaries and Intelligence Summaries are contained in F. S. Regs., Part II, and the Staff Manual respectively. Title pages will be prepared in manuscript.

| Hour, Date, Place. | Summary of Events and Information. | Remarks and references to Appendices. |
|---|---|---|
| CHLORITE. | | |
| 8.7.15. | Capt F.J. ANDERSON I.M.S. reported this return from temporary duty with 34th PIONEERS. | fm. |
| 9.7.15. | Capt C H REINHOLD I.M.S. returned from a weeks leave. | fm. |
| 10.7.15 | Weather cool & cloudy. | |
| 11.7.15 | The mail-corren under orders of ADMS arrived this date — and turned today in review where was examined an an likely to be fit for duty again in a fortnight to 3 weeks. 38 truck were returned from hosp & J.R.A. Major A. MELHUIST I.M.S. reported his departure on one month's leave. Lt. J.C. JOHN Qurs. reg. owned from hospital duty with - to 112 J.R.A. | appr. |
| 12.7.15. | Under orders from ADMS Meerut Div, carry of Infection Diseases Section are not to be admitted to this hospital & all patients admitted on "maintre" from other Field Ambulances & sent down on first afternoon | appr. |
| 13.7.15. | 10 cases discharged to transferred & 10 admitted | appr. |

# WAR DIARY
## or
## INTELLIGENCE SUMMARY.

(Erase heading not required.)

Army Form C. 2118.

| Hour, Date, Place. | Summary of Events and Information. | Remarks and references to Appendices. |
|---|---|---|
| CHOLONNE 14.7.15. | 40 patients admitted today on transfer. The 4 new English Sabbon Spinsbey Hints have erected today no work. Each takes 16 patients comfortably. Heavy rain at night, felt the tents proved quite waterproof. | |
| 15.7.15. | Reply letter from ADMS to 24/76 of 13.7.15. 4 Horse Ambulances were sent away from the unit to be allotted to other formations. Our Ambulance Transport now consists of 2 Horse Ambulances & one Motor Ambulance in charge of Corporal & 3 Drivers during fatigue 86. 11 patients admitted on transfer. Admitted 5 pts. Discharged 5 pts. Remaining 86. | OCR OCR |
| 16.7.15. 17.7.15. | Weather cold with stormy wind + frequent showers. The new huts are satisfactory under these trying weather conditions. Admitted 15 pts. Discharged 6. Transferred to Casualty Clearing Station 2. Remaining 95. | OCR. |
| 18.7.15. | MAJOR H. MELLWISH reported his return from our home leave. Patients admitted 6. Discharges to Conv. H. Transferred to Casualty Clearing Station 2. Remaining 95. Weather fine & warmer. | Som |

Army Form C. 2118.

# WAR DIARY
## or
## INTELLIGENCE SUMMARY.

*(Erase heading not required.)*

99.

| Hour, Date, Place. | Summary of Events and Information. | Remarks and references to Appendices. |
|---|---|---|
| CAMNE. 19.7.15 | Admitted 12. Discharged 10 July 2. Remaining 104 | 15m. |
| 20.7.15. | Colnl. D.C. V. FITZGERALD returned from 8 days one one weeks leave. Admitted 11. Discharge 9. Remaining 106. | 15m. |
| 21.7.15. | Admitted 55. Discharges 106 reg 1. transferred to Casualty Clearing Station 3. Remaining 157. An asoutnend been has been taken over we counted an unusual influx of 32 patients. | 15m. |
| 22.7.15. | Admitted 9. Transferred to C.C.S. Meerut 1. Remaining 165. Weather variable. Intermittent rain. | 15m. |
| 23.7.15. | Admitted 17. Discharge 1 to Dy 15. transferred to C.C.S 2. Remaining 165. Weather variable Stormy. | 15m. |
| 24.7.15. | Admitted 14. Discharged to duty 5. transferred to CCS 8. 2. Remaining 172. | 15m. |
| 25.7.15. | Admitted 4 Transferred to C.C.S 2. To duty 2. Remaining 172. | 15m. |

Gulab Singh & Sons, Calcutta—No. 22 Army C—5-8-14—1,07,000.

**Army Form C. 2118.**

# WAR DIARY
## or
## INTELLIGENCE SUMMARY.
*(Erase heading not required.)*

Instructions regarding War Diaries and Intelligence Summaries are contained in F. S. Regs., Part II, and the Staff Manual respectively. Title pages will be prepared in manuscript.

| Hour, Date, Place. | Summary of Events and Information. | Remarks and references to Appendices. |
|---|---|---|
| ESTAIRES 26.2.15 | The Field Ambulances marched at 12 noon to ESTAIRES via MERVILLE & LAGORGUE arriving at 2 p.m. 184 Cars were transported in 15 motor & horse ambulances which were borrowed from various units of the LAHORE & MEERUT Divisions. On arrival in ESTAIRES the ambulances proceeded to occupy distributing of the École Filles du Sacré Cœur in the RUE COLLÉGE taking on from the 1/2 HIGHLAND FIELD AMBULANCE of the 51st HIGHLAND Division. Wards were arranged in various rooms of the school & being in the neighbourhood of 3 in the avenues, in which were also localled the officers quarters. | Map. FRANCE 36A L 29 & 1/5. |

Army Form C. 2118.

# WAR DIARY
## or
## INTELLIGENCE SUMMARY.

(Erase heading not required.)

101

| Hour, Date, Place. | Summary of Events and Information. | Remarks and references to Appendices. |
|---|---|---|
| ESTAIRES 26-7-15 | On the main building a supply receiving Pack & two offices were established. On the upper carpark of the building cleaning the ground of its almost unlimited patients already assailed. Tents were pitched in a neighbouring field for the accommodation of further suspects. In may 12 weeks have been taken (deal with 300 patients) & they are quite sufficient - blankets & some water drawn in tankers were unloaded & stored in the cellar of the ambulance. It continued for a long time personnel is a tremendous strain on it. The staff disbelect that its necessary materially the incalculable with the building. A great reserve in the building were responsible for | |

Army Form C. 2118.

# WAR DIARY
## or
## INTELLIGENCE SUMMARY.

(Erase heading not required.)

102.

| Hour, Date, Place. | Summary of Events and Information. | Remarks and references to Appendices. |
|---|---|---|
| ESTAIRES 26.7.15. | None of the school staff sisters were visited to lunch. The movements of the patients who entered & departed afford the undermentioned conclusion. Cases admitted 18 — Remaining 190 | |
| 27.7.15. | Admitted 15. Transferred to C.C.S. 19.2. Capt. Highbrals reported. Transferred to Works. S. Transferred Remaining 201. | 2 weeks leave. |
| 28.7.15. | Admitted 11. C.C.S. 3. Capt. F.S. Anderson reported his departure on one weeks leave. | |
| 29.7.15. | Admitted 19. to C.C.S. 8. Transferred to own Hosp. 6. to C.C.S. 5. bearer Sd. four remaining 185. | |
| 30.7.15. | Admitted 22. Discharged to duty 6. to C.C.S.S. Remaining 196. The Ambulance was visited by Surg. General MacPhersn KMS + Su B Lieutenant. | |

Gulab Singh & Sons, Calcutta—No. 22 Army G—5-8-14—1,07,000.

Army Form C. 2118.

# WAR DIARY
## or
## INTELLIGENCE SUMMARY.
*(Erase heading not required.)*

103

| Hour, Date, Place. | Summary of Events and Information. | Remarks and references to Appendices. |
|---|---|---|
| ESTAIRES 31-7-15. | Admitted 17. Discharged to Duty 17 - to days to Casualty Clearing Station 13 - Remaining 183. Weather fine and warm. | 1Ph. |

S Maxwell Major
g/me
Commdg.

Serial No 153

121/6958

13/4/48

Aug/15

# WAR DIARY
## OF
### 111th Indian Field Ambulance

FROM 1st August 1915 TO 31st August 1915

Army Form C. 2118

# WAR DIARY
## or
## INTELLIGENCE SUMMARY.
### Vol XII
(Erase heading not required.)

Instructions regarding War Diaries and Intelligence Summaries are contained in F. S. Regs., Part II. and the Staff Manual respectively. Title pages will be prepared in manuscript.

| Hour, Date, Place. | Summary of Events and Information. | Remarks and references to Appendices. |
|---|---|---|
| ESTAIRES 1-8-15. | Admitted O. Transferred to Torsmays MERVILLE H3. Transferred 113 I.F.A. 140. The ambulance closed for sick. Capt. D.C.V. Fitzgerald I.M.S. left for temporary duty with 15 Sikhs. | Kr |
| 2-8-15. | The Field Ambulance marched from ESTAIRES at 2 pm & proceeded via the ESTAIRES — BETHUNE road to LE LOBES. arriving there at 4 pm & training for sick of the Reserve Brigade in the Shed attached to the right of the LE LOBES — VIELLE CHAPELLE road. Accommodation on Ground floor for 9 to the 1st floor for 35 patients. Comfortably. | MAP. FRANCE 36A R.27.6.-1/5  MAP  Kr |

# WAR DIARY

## INTELLIGENCE SUMMARY

| Hour, Date, Place. | Summary of Events and Information. | Remarks and references to Appendices. |
|---|---|---|
| ZELOBES | | |
| 3-8-15 | Admitted 8. Transferred to C.C.S. 5 including one case of suspected Cholera - final diag. Running 4. | pm |
| 4-8-15 | Capt. J.F. Anderson IMS returned from leave. Admitted 4. Transferred to C.C.S. 1. Running 7. | am |
| 5-8-15 | Lieut J.C.Jolly reported his departure on weeks leave. Admitted 9. Transferred to C.C.S. 3. Running 13. Capt A.C.V. Fitzgerald returned from temporary duty with the 15th Sikhs. | am |
| 6-8-15 | Admitted 10. Transferred to C.C.S. 5. Running 18. Heather, S.W.Tr. during staying. | pm |
| 7-8-15 | Admitted 6. Transferred to C.C.S. 5. Running 7. Sick on leaving calculated from 40th Pathans 5, Rifles 4, 19 Sikhs 4, 34 Pioneers 2, 21st Coy Sappers Miners 1, 15th Sikhs dept 1. The enclosed copy of Cochin found manuscript forward with Sivanan on 3-8-15 has been deposed as such | pm |

# WAR DIARY or INTELLIGENCE SUMMARY.

Army Form C. 2118.

106.

Instructions regarding War Diaries and Intelligence Summaries are contained in F. S. Regs., Part II, and the Staff Manual respectively. Title pages will be prepared in manuscript.

(Erase heading not required.)

| Hour, Date, Place. | Summary of Events and Information. | Remarks and references to Appendices. |
|---|---|---|
| ZELORES 8-8-15 | Admitted 20. Transferred 2. Remaining 35. Several cases of Conjunctivitis having occurred slides were examined & pneumococci found. The O.C. Causalities Laboratory (Kirk) visited the hospital today to make a fuller examination and take smears & some culture tubes. Duties normal. | m. |
| 9.8.15. | Admitted 9. including the case of accidental G.S.W. left knee 15th Sikhs. Transferred to CCS 13. Remaining 2+. 2/Lt. E.L. WAINWRIGHT admitted suffering from Jaundice. Transferred to No 2 C.C.S. The ambulance lorries which have been inflated with rice, are now pleated & another stretcher across the lorries frame. | m. |
| 10-8-15. | Admitted 4. Transferred to C.C.S. 2. Remaining 26. The SIRHIND Brigade having been relieved by the branches of the TURUNDOR Brigade, sick were collected from Regiments of the former | |

Army Form C. 2118

# WAR DIARY
or
## INTELLIGENCE SUMMARY.
(Erase heading not required.)

107

Instructions regarding War Diaries and Intelligence Summaries are contained in F.S. Regs., Part II, and the Staff Manual respectively. Title pages will be prepared in manuscript.

| Hour, Date, Place. | Summary of Events and Information. | Remarks and references to Appendices. |
|---|---|---|
| LAHORE<br>10-8-15. | We ordered into Reserve. Strength - 11/8 GURKHAS 15th SIKHS - 11/4th in addition from the 34th PIONEERS + 21st Coy. SAPPERS+MINERS. These latter have been visited daily by our M.O. from this unit - for infection of Carolina Spinal Contacts. | 18m. |
| 11-8-15. | Admitted 2 - Discharged to duty 2. Transferred to C.C.S 4 - Remained 22. Station warm + fine | 5m. |
| 12-8-15. | Lt. T.C. John reported Re Relieved from one week's leave. Admitted 3 - Discharge to duty 1. Transferred to C.C.S 4. Remained 20 Completed 6 Transfer reasoned 112 I.F.A. 3 Transferred to C.C.S 2 - Remaining 27. | 4m. |
| 13-8-15 | One Ambulance transp. for wounded, taking over the Sec. V.A.S.T. Pol.t from No. 112 I.F.A. the at 3-30 p.m., and the duties of clearing the |  |

# WAR DIARY or INTELLIGENCE SUMMARY

Army Form C. 2118

108

| Hour, Date, Place. | Summary of Events and Information. | Remarks and references to Appendices. |
|---|---|---|
| LE LOBES 13-8-15 | Front line extending from the ESTAIRES – LA BASSÉE road on the left to BOND STREET on the right held by the TURUNDUR Bridge being one battalion. An Armoured Train drawing Rations formed at St VAAST POST by CAPT D.C.V. FITZ-GERALD IMS the following Personnel & equipment were left there – S.A.S. TEK CHAND and men orderly, 1st section of the Bearer Division – half of equipment of the Bearer Division with an additional supply of dressings, Shell dressings, Iodine Ampoules, Morphia Nitrate and Ammonia Capsules. A platoon of Gurkhas we taken over from No 112 I.F.A. Don Kahars and milk stretchers were sent to the support of MANCHESTERS. 4/15 SIKHS + 59th RIFLES. CAPT FITZGERALD visited trenches at 10–11 am collected wounded. |  |

# WAR DIARY
## INTELLIGENCE SUMMARY.

*(Erase heading not required.)*

Army Form C. 2118.

109.

| Hour, Date, Place. | Summary of Events and Information. | Remarks and references to Appendices. |
|---|---|---|
| ZELOBES 14-8-15 | Admitted 29 transfer rec'd 9. Transferred to C.C.S 6. Died 1. Remaining 58. | |
| 15-8-15. | Admitted 24. Transferred to C.C.S. 20 in 2 days. July 2 Remaining 60 – Lieut. John Img visited the stevenson group station at 10 P.m. to collect wounded. 16 Indian bearers were taken on from No 113 I.F.A. to transport in Field work & set to St VAAST hut to meet Sgt-TECK CHAND. They appear to be a steady body of men. The members of the International Commission headed by Prof. NEWSTEAD violated its fate Ambulance in the afternoon to trace an infection of the lines, anxious by mosquitoes. For fly-breeding purposes. More could be found. The half filled pounds were & they have been flies (thanks to the |  |

| Hour, Date, Place. | Summary of Events and Information. | Remarks and references to Appendices. |
|---|---|---|
| LE LOBES 15-8-15 | Aircraft manner in which all latter night shell & other refuse matter is incinerated. Attempts to large numbers of flies are successfully found. Also of the asphyxiating fumes which these live in an accumulating condition. The sanitary officer accurately headed places consist of the commissioners revealed the located. The Commissioners revealed the use of hurricles of a sample which walls others sufferers were flies to affect at a bugle noise rather than stiff from Mafeusis. heretho showing. 10 h. | |
| 16-8-15. | Admitted 26 Transferred to C.C.S. 6 Discharged to Duty 2. Remaining 70. Capt RE IN NO 13 visited the sepharehal air to be called forward at 11 hrs. | 10 h. 4 Ph. |

# WAR DIARY
## or
## INTELLIGENCE SUMMARY

Army Form C. 2118

111

| Hour, Date, Place. | Summary of Events and Information. | Remarks and references to Appendices. |
|---|---|---|
| ZBLORGES 17-8-15. | Capt. FITZGERALD visited the Advanced Collecting Post at 10-30 pm to collect wounded. 2nd Class No. 346. S.A.S DAULAT RAM reported his arrival for temporary duty. A heavy thunder storm passed over the ambulance at midday and continuing the East. Surveying the last nils of Sunken road, the road & tramway staff, & tramways were considerably well & Cjnds to managed it. Sixteen other ranks picked up here. Three admitted to us — including one officer, transferred to C.C.S. 18. Transferred (SM 1135)A 7, Discharged to duty 2. Remaining 55. | |
| 18-8-15. | Capt Anderson visited the Advanced Post. 10-30 pm then the Advanced wounded. | |

Army Form C. 2118

# WAR DIARY
## or
## INTELLIGENCE SUMMARY.
*(Erase heading not required.)*

Instructions regarding War Diaries and Intelligence Summaries are contained in F. S. Regs., Part II, and the Staff Manual respectively. Title pages will be prepared in manuscript.

112

| Hour, Date, Place. | Summary of Events and Information. | Remarks and references to Appendices. |
|---|---|---|
| ZELOBES 19-8-15. | Resit John visited the asphodic at 10-30 hrs weekdelowmded. There was a wounded internment in the centre, afterwards lain of the present day. | |
| 20-8-15. | Capt. REINFORD visited the advanced dressing station at 10 hrs to select ground for his station, while a party of helpers, including 16 Nks S. VAAST Padre relief from the one at the Asylum. These stretcher shelters were hit. All more or less unsuitable. There of the shelters proceeded unmolested to the screening station about 400 lands distant before me help which was immediately and. They were served on fresh of Sinistery to the field Ambulance were also found necessary. I Severali two of the injured men along with C.C.S. MERVILLE | 4tm. |

# WAR DIARY or INTELLIGENCE SUMMARY.

(Erase heading not required.)

Army Form C. 2118

13.

| Hour, Date, Place. | Summary of Events and Information. | Remarks and references to Appendices. |
|---|---|---|
| JELOBES 21-8-15. | The field ambulances as well as the Advanced Dressing Stations were inspected today by the D.M.S. Reserve accompanied by Sir W. LEISHMAN, the D.D.M.S. Indian Corps, the A.D.M.S. LAHORE DIVISION. The A.M.S. Reserve afterwards inspected with the General Arrangements of the hospital. | Rm. |
| 22-8-15. | Capt. Fitzgerald visited the posts along our front for the purpose of collecting wounded. Instructions of the A.D.M.S. have been issued for the practice of collecting wounded to the form up daylight, as there is much safety by the construction of Communication Trenches between Dressing Stations & outposts. | Rm. |
| 23-8-15. | Capt. Anderson visited the aid posts at 5 a.m. & collected wounded. | Rm. |

Army Form C. 2118

# WAR DIARY
or
## INTELLIGENCE SUMMARY.
(Erase heading not required.)

Instructions regarding War Diaries and Intelligence
Summaries are contained in F. S. Regs., Part II,
and the Staff Manual respectively. Title pages
will be prepared in manuscript.

114.

| Hour, Date, Place. | Summary of Events and Information. | Remarks and references to Appendices. |
|---|---|---|
| ZELOBES 24-8-15. | Lt. Joffre visited the outpost at 6 a.m. Major Methuish visited the advanced dressing station & toured part of the 47th Sikhs with Pervey. | Jm. |
| 25-8-15. | Capt. Rawford visited the outpost at 6 a.m. In the morning the Field ambulance was inspected by Col Pike, S.D. M.S. Indian Corps. | Jm. |
| 26-8-15. | Capt. Fitzgerald visited the outpost at 6 a.m. | Jm. |
| 27-8-15. | Capt. Augerson visited the outpost at 6 am. At 10 p.m. orders Methuish and head-Joffre visited Stewart and one post of the position of the outpost of the 55th Punjabis who have just come into the line. Joffre & were left at the infantry brigade outpost as Lt. Joffre ill. Capt. Fitzgerald Lt. Vance took part. | Jm. |

Gulab Singh & Sons, Calcutta—No. 22 Army C.—5-8-14—1,07,000.

Army Form C. 2118

115.

# WAR DIARY
or
INTELLIGENCE SUMMARY.

(Erase heading not required.)

| Hour, Date, Place. | Summary of Events and Information. | Remarks and references to Appendices. |
|---|---|---|
| ZEROBES 28-8-15. | Lieut. J. C. JOHN returned at HQ Referenced Drawing Station | |
| 29-8-15 | Major MELTHUISH and Capt. REINHOLD visited SVAAST post at 10 a.m. A rearrangement of posts in the front line resulting in the occupation of the Lahore Dismounted forage godown on the right of no. 6 post of the Lahore tramway, front of Station at the Grau farm to the Meerut tramway the centre in one on one left. A continued advance during station at St Vaast Post has accordingly been found by bringing the 8 BFA the Coylon funishing a post of 1 Sowary order hastening, Afridies, 1 Sheik of Cook together with A Cullew armament, equipment & such like supplies enforce one tent Comforts | |

# WAR DIARY
## INTELLIGENCE SUMMARY
*(Erase heading not required.)*

Army Form C. 2118

116

| Hour, Date, Place. | Summary of Events and Information. | Remarks and references to Appendices. |
|---|---|---|
| 2.0 P.M. 29-8-15 | Emergency leaving the G.M.O. remains on duty all the pce for 24 hours. Ambulances obtained from the two field Ambulances wagons are being collected from the following regts for the return from the post being detailed to duty at each outpost. Connaught Rangers, 1st Londons (?), D.G. Bhils, 9th Punjabis. | M. |
| 30-8-15 | On afternoon V.8.8 of the Sir Pertal . . . | |
| 31-8-15 | Capt Fitzgerald proceeds by the Renown to Hospital Station for 24 hours duty. Two field Ambulances and Ry wagons are invited . by the beaunit Section on Army Cope accompanied D.M.S. Irwin KMS & Lt Col Morgan R.A.M.C. | M. |

S. Mahmood Mozaffar OC 111 S.F.A.

Sept. 1915
121/7286
Serial No. 153.

# Confidential

121/7286

## War Diary

*with appendices.*

of

___ III Indian Field Ambulance ___

FROM 1st September 1915. TO 30th September 1915.

Army Form C. 2118.

## MAJOR MELHUISH'S WAR DIARY

or

## INTELLIGENCE SUMMARY.

VOL XIII

(Erase heading not required.)

| Hour, Date, Place. | Summary of Events and Information. | Remarks and references to Appendices. |
|---|---|---|
| 7 LOBES 1-9-15. | Major MELHUISH accompanied the ADMS LAHORE Division on a visit to the LAHORE Cavalry Station in the afternoon. A telegram was made to some neighbouring homes for suitable site for another Cavalry Station to be used in times of emergency. | R 27 C 1.4 FRANCE BETHUNE (conduct sheet) M. |
| 2-9-15. | Major MELHUISH accompanied the ADMS LAHORE Division on a visit to the Advanced training Station to wheel-hundury operations & the Remount Station on the ALBERT Road. Colr. ANDERSON was on duty at Remount fort. MUBAREAK ALI sits No 2258 Sofa MZIR INGRAIN two deaths occurred in the day, were with the Cavalry behind near of the Co Punjabs No 2250 Sepoy SHAH. They were buried in the Civilian Burial ground. | M. |
| 3-9-15. | Major MELHUISH & Capt. FITZGERALD visited the site of the new Remount Station on Albert Road to arrange to pitch tents for Cavalry Coolies. | M. |

# WAR DIARY or INTELLIGENCE SUMMARY

Army Form C. 2118.

*(Erase heading not required.)*

Instructions regarding War Diaries and Intelligence Summaries are contained in F. S. Regs., Part II, and the Staff Manual respectively. Title pages will be prepared in manuscript.

| Hour, Date, Place. | Summary of Events and Information. | Remarks and references to Appendices. |
|---|---|---|
| ZEROES 4-9-15 | Capt. FITZGERALD spent day making dug out & improving the protection of dug out at ALBERT Road, which is to be used as an Armoured Electric but Treasury. Naik TOHN was on duty at Kashafpur. The neighbourhood of which was shelled fairly heavily during the day. Two shells burst apparently at an observation balloon fell about 500 yards short of the tent. Division. | JM. |
| 5-9-15 | Capt. FITZGERALD completed the dug out at ALBERT Road. No 1909 Hav. BHAN SINGH of 85 E PUNJABIS died of illness in hospital. | JM. |
| 6-9-15 | Capt. REINHOLD was on duty at the Armoured Train Station. The work of rebuilding the Surfing & constructing new hidden works in support area is proceeding. Contractor JM. |

Army Form C. 2118.

# WAR DIARY
## or
## INTELLIGENCE SUMMARY.

*(Erase heading not required.)*

119.

| Hour, Date, Place. | Summary of Events and Information. | Remarks and references to Appendices. |
|---|---|---|
| LEMNOS — 7-9-15. | Capt. FITZGERALD visited the Collecting Station at ALBERT Road and also a stretcher which will take for Rehab and dressings brought up from the S.S. PUNTARSIS & convey them to the Princess Beaming Station. Sick were collected today from the S.S. PUNTARSIS, just arrived from EGYPT. | |
| 8-9-15. | I visited St. Vincent fort accompanied by the A.D.M.S. I inspected the work which has been done on the house, everything in order. Only stragglers were on duty there during the day. Practically their neighborhood & no disturbance of the daily routine during the holiday or life. | |
| 9-9-15. | Again visited S. Vincent fort. Visited the work in progress. | |

# WAR DIARY
## or
## INTELLIGENCE SUMMARY.
(Erase heading not required.)

Army Form C. 2118.

| Hour, Date, Place. | Summary of Events and Information. | Remarks and references to Appendices. |
|---|---|---|
| TELOBES 10-9-15. | Colo- ANDERSON was on duty at the Browncad Training Station.— Major MELHUISH accompanied Lt. H. M. Patons in his visit of Shrapnel in testing & inspect the progress of work | Jm. |
| 11-9-15. | Routine. D. John was on duty at the Advanced Training Station. | Jm. |
| 13-9-15. | Routine. | Jm. |
| 14-9-15. | Capt. Rainhos has on duty at Ft. Howard Training Station in which he visited in the evening & Major Melhuish & Colr. Fitzgerald. | Jm. |
| 15-9-15. | Draz Kahan belonging to No 8 BSA were admitted suffering from shell wounds which they received while at work on road repairs near Carmor Bridge Station. Wharves wounds were very slight. Jm. | |

Army Form C. 2118.

# WAR DIARY
## or
## INTELLIGENCE SUMMARY.

(Erase heading not required.)

Instructions regarding War Diaries and Intelligence Summaries are contained in F. S. Regs., Part II, and the Staff Manual respectively. Title pages will be prepared in manuscript.

121.

| Hour, Date, Place. | Summary of Events and Information. | Remarks and references to Appendices. |
|---|---|---|
| JEROBES. 16-9-15. | Capt. Fitzgerald was on duty at the Advanced Dressing Station where he was engaged in re-roofing the Kalara Quarters. | JM. |
| 17-9-15. | Routine. | JM. |
| 18-9-15. | Capt ANDERSON I.M.S was on duty at the Advanced Dressing Station. no occurrence. | JM. |
| 19-9-15. | An interesting case was admitted during the day, No 47 Hav AITHAM KHAN 56 RIFLES(F.F.) was hit by a rifle-bullet on the river. The bullet first hulas the bone the entrance was on the back of thorax to the left of the middle line. the bullet having apparently missed the Great soft arteries, lungs, skull & Spinal cord & all important structures on the way. So far the man is quite all right. The Symptoms beyond slight difficulty in breathing & little Spirited blood in the Sputa & mere letters - 24hrs. | JM. |

Gulab Singh & Sons, Calcutta—No. 22 Army C.—5-8-14—1,07,000.

# WAR DIARY or INTELLIGENCE SUMMARY.

*(Erase heading not required.)*

Army Form C. 2118.

122.

| Hour, Date, Place. | Summary of Events and Information. | Remarks and references to Appendices. |
|---|---|---|
| IERES 20-9-15. | Lt. JOHN. was on duty at the Advanced Dressing Station. | |
| 21-9-15. | Routine. | |
| 22-9-15 | Cpl. REINFORD was on duty at the Advanced Dressing Station. Cpl. Fitzgerald was employed throughout the day in collecting supplies board at various points; also on the relief line intended to direct wounded stragglers to the Dressing Station. | |
| 23-9-15. | 50 Army Bearers having completed work on shelters at St Vaast Post were withdrawn to Brewery barracks. | |
| 24-9-15 | Shrader orders received from the Front line where from men the Bearers brought in were Cpl. FITZGERALD I.M.S. turned out & the Advanced Dressing Station, at noon made out of list of missing personnel. Sgn. 15th BC OC | |

**Army Form C. 2118.**

# WAR DIARY
## or
## INTELLIGENCE SUMMARY.

(Erase heading not required.)

| Hour, Date, Place. | Summary of Events and Information. | Remarks and references to Appendices. |
|---|---|---|
| LELOBES 24-9-15 | Lt. L. C. JOHN IMS. S.A.S. KARTAR RAM who travel ordinarily with 50 Bearers S.Ks HARNAM SINGH with 50 Bearers was already on the spot. The following personnel & equipment from Allahabad Ambulances reported available for duty :— 1 Cap. 2 Bay 3 me Lt — A KENNEDY IMS. Lt. 112 I.F.A.:— Lt. Entrale surgeon 3 beds Orderlies. 90 Bearers, 4 me Lieut Ambulance Lieut 112 I.F.A.:— Cafe. RT. NELIS. IMS. 1 Lt. Surgeon. 1 Suft. & 160 Shutia Bearers — 9 Horse Ambulances — 2 Motor Ambulances. Lahore Ambulances. 1 Lt. 2 Bay. 2 Section :— Two RAMC Orderlies. 1 clerk on telephone, orderlies & stretcher bearers. Storing. 10 followed on marching Status, & stretchers. 2 dis-tributed to units for defence of ammunition Convoy available. 2 Medical Officers reported to the Convoy. FITZGERALD'S Mule with Lt JOHN. (Capt. NELIS & Sub. Amb. from 2 hospitals field Ambulances 2 horse, ambulance 1 Horse (Mule or Pony) |   |

# WAR DIARY
## or
## INTELLIGENCE SUMMARY

Army Form C. 2118.

| Hour, Date, Place. | Summary of Events and Information. | Remarks and references to Appendices. |
|---|---|---|
| Lahore S. 24-5-15. | 1.2. to Bearers taken to were British - with a sufficient Comp.(?) of transport - without transport drivers - MATHEWHURST I.M.S. CAPT REINHOLD I.M.S. CAPT. J.F.BOYD I.M.S. CAPT J.J. ANDERSON I.M.S. & Lt. KENNEDY I.M.S. accompany Lt. P. de SOUSA who reported his arrival with the convoy, & 3 Sub. Asst. Surgeons + quartermasters. Of 15 motor ambulances available 3 were sold to St Andrew's Field Ambulance before its line from the front these two motor ambulances were held by the FEROZEPORE BRIGADE. Composed of the following personnel - 10 Gurkhas from 6th & 57th, the Lights Brigade, Connaughts, 5th Bombay Lt. Inf. to the enemy + 57 Stretcher (FA) in reserve. One word here in the hands of Capt FITZGERALD I.M.S. whose report on the operations is attached. |  |

# WAR DIARY or INTELLIGENCE SUMMARY

Army Form C. 2118.

125

| Hour, Date, Place. | Summary of Events and Information. | Remarks and references to Appendices. |
|---|---|---|
| LE ROBES 24-9-15 | Collection of wounded from the TUNING OR before Béthune began at a late hour of the ESTAIRES-LA BASSÉE road was performed by the 3 sections of No 8 B.F.A. working from their advanced dressing station at M 27 d 5/6 — More wounded from the Regiment were carried in motor ambulances of No 8 B.F.A. & the Field Ambulances. Civilian manner British wounded & the prisoners before passing on to a Ci- were evacuated in motor ambulances to the 8 B.F.A. Distribution at VIEILLE CHAPELLE R 95 d 111. By the action of fog & artillery fire was of a wooden frame used together & the distribution before and at the defending on & various heavy rain [?] houses in the neighborhood had the [?] information had been upstairs [?] accumulate | BÉTHUNE (Gardenies [?] Sheet) 1/40000 |

Army Form C. 2118.

# WAR DIARY
## or
## INTELLIGENCE SUMMARY.

(Erase heading not required.)

Instructions regarding War Diaries and Intelligence Summaries are contained in F. S. Regs., Part II and the Staff Manual respectively. Title pages will be prepared in manuscript.

| Hour, Date, Place. | Summary of Events and Information. | Remarks and references to Appendices. |
|---|---|---|
|  TENCHES 24-9-15 | Upwards of 250 batch of wounded were admitted during the afternoon from 5.30pm to 5am on the 25. All medical Officers & mobiles were transferred to No 112 J.F.A at CROIX MARMUSE. | |
| 25-9-15. | At 6am the first ambulance wagons were sent to [illeg] at a previously selected point M 36 a 6/8. It was intended to send slightly wounded men capable of standing the fatigue of a shell jolt under charge of Rakus by the wheeled field ambulance wagons to this point, from whence they could be conveyed in the motor wagons to the rear. It was only found necessary to carry one wagon load in this fashion. | M. |

Gulab Singh & Sons, Calcutta—No, 22 Army C.—5-8-14—1,07,000.

**Army Form C. 2118.**

# WAR DIARY
## or
## INTELLIGENCE SUMMARY.
*(Erase heading not required.)*

107.

| Hour, Date, Place. | Summary of Events and Information. | Remarks and references to Appendices. |
|---|---|---|
| ZELOBES. 25-9-15 | On the lines indicated above & in Appendix H. 93 wounded were cleared to the Divisional train of F.A's during the day, the majority of them in the morning. No tent or motor ambulances were held at the A.D.S. nor field ambulances in the immediate vicinity— as the A.D.M.S. had been informed that no casualties were likely up till that point. Road from the right of the line Cape WELLS - I.M.S. who had been stationed at CHOCOLATE MENIER CORNER was withdrawn to the Division — Kahars were however left there as at the collecting station in HAZEBROEK ROAD.<br>At 6 pm the horse ambulances were withdrawn from the rendezvous here, it not being thought that the further | See Appendix H.<br>O.W.Fitzgerald's Report |

At M 36 a.6 heavy firing....

# WAR DIARY
## or
## INTELLIGENCE SUMMARY

Army Form C. 2118.

128.

| Hour, Date, Place. | Summary of Events and Information. | Remarks and references to Appendices. |
|---|---|---|
| LAHORE<br>25-9-15 | The following wagons were classed these lines & cars of No XII MAC from St. VENANT, and has never more than half full. Of the 131 casualties received during the 24th 9 25th inst. seventy nine were wounded men & of the 115 Brandenburghers suffering from venereal Brandenburghers below the usual orders men cases were from Lahore known the men were not evacuated Division. McLeavonel Crescent Station with the others, but were detained pending enquiry. | |
| 26-9-15 | Evacuation of wounded from the hospital continued during the day; 58 wounded | |
| 27-9-15 | All lighting in the hospitals having been scaled last night & there being no prospect of early renewal, it was decided | |

Army Form C. 2118.

# WAR DIARY
## or
## INTELLIGENCE SUMMARY.

129.

(Erase heading not required.)

| Hour, Date, Place. | Summary of Events and Information. | Remarks and references to Appendices. |
|---|---|---|
| LECODES. 27-8-15. | Galleur all essential personnel and materiel to new Dressing station; with the exception that the Shelters of 113 I.F.A. & Capt. WELLS I.M.S were retained. Lt. JOHN I.M.S. was relieved of the advanced Dressing Capt. ANDERSON I.M.S. relieved Capt. FITZGERALD at the advanced Dressing Section this morning. 34 wounded were admitted during the day. Evacd. | M |
| 28-8-15 | Capt. WELLS I.M.S. & Lt. British Bearer relieved of 113 I.F.A. — There are no wounded for attention. Ambulances formed with unit. was admitted during the day 10 wounded. | M |
| 29-8-15 | The F.A. ambulance received orders for heavier cargo. RC John relieved Capt. ANDERSON at the A. Dressing Station. | M |

Army Form C. 2118.

# WAR DIARY
## or
## INTELLIGENCE SUMMARY.
*(Erase heading not required.)*

130

| Hour, Date, Place. | Summary of Events and Information. | Remarks and references to Appendices. |
|---|---|---|
| ZELOBES 30-9-15. | Routine. The weather during recent operations has been bad after the first day (29/9) heavy rain showers occurring at more or less short intervals. | Appendix 2. Col: T.C. Johns's report. |

S Mackintosh Majr
OC 1119FA

Appendix T (re mid-# Sept. Ger...) 16

Report on the work of the Advanced Dressing Station and Bearer Divn 111 / 2 FD from 24.9.15 to 26.9.15.

The area dealt with by this unit extends from the ESTAIRES–LA BASEE Rd to the extreme right of the trenches held by the Ferozepore Bde, the position of the regimental aid posts being as follows:—

4th Suffolks. LANSDOWN POST.
129th by the end of the tram line on
    the RUE DU BOIS, approximately S.10.a.
Connaught Rangers. On the EDWARD Rd
    near the RUE DU BOIS. S.9.
57th In reserve trenches behind RUE
    DU BOIS between ALBERT & EDWARD Rd
89th In support trenches on the right
    in front of the RUE DU BOIS to the
    right of the end of EDWARD Rd.

The regiment holding the last named position was previously evacuating their wounded via the CADBURY communication trench to CHOCOLATE CORNER from whence they were conveyed to the

Advanced dressing station on the ALBERT RD. For this purpose Bearers were posted at CHOCOLATE CORNER and at a collecting station established on the ALBERT RD at S.8.b.4.6. This arrangement was altered on the 24th inst and a new collecting station started on the RUE DU BOIS at S.9.c.8.8. An old dug out behind a house was here hurriedly sandbagged & protected as far as possible. A guard over 12 bearers were posted here to deal with cases from the 89th who were brought to them from the right and put via the PALL MALL comn. trench. The M.O. was notified as to the position of this collecting station.

The M.Os of each unit except the 57th were visited during the 24th and requested to send information of any change in the position of their aid posts either to the collecting stations or to the dressing station.

A rendezvous for horse ambulances has been selected at M 36 a.6.8. A march & 4 bearers were stationed a short cut by a field path

at this point by which were
proposed to cross parties of slightly
wounded casualties.

During the afternoon the staff at
the dressing station was increased
by personnel from other units, the
total strength being:

M.O. 3
Asst Surgeon 1.
Sub Asst Surgeon 3.
Staff Sergeant 1.    (in charge of Bhisties)
Barric orderlies 2.   (for telephone duty)
Ward orderlies 2.
Bhisties      1
Cooks         1
Sweepers      5
Naicks a.b.c  5
Kahars 22 9 (including Bhisties)

Additional motor ambulances were also
detailed for duty at the dressing station.

In order to prevent casualties
from straying from the divisional
area, Kahars were left at
Chocolate menu and at the ALBERT
Rd collecting station, the evacuation
by this route being supervised by

Capt. WELLS. 2nd and Lieutenant
PINTO.

The original number of Askaris at
each aid post was doubled during the
night of the 24th 25th, except in the
case of the 89th & 57th who were
served by the collecting stations

During the night of the 24th 25th 17
casualties were brought in, none
being of a serious nature.
Before daylight on the 25th 2nd asst.
Surgeon ALI. JAN and 20 additional
askaris were posted to the new
collecting station on the RUE DU BOIS,
a novice & 20 Askaris were taken
by CAPT WELLS to evacuate
casualties by the ALBERT Rd route.
A novice and 20 Askaris were
detailed for duty at the end of the
tram line where six trollies had
been left during the night.
I first visited the new collecting
station and then proceeded to
the 123rd aid post.
It had been decided to relieve
the 125th by the 57th and this
was done during the early morning

of the 21st. The advance party of the
129th has been moved to
LANSDOWN post with part of the
regiment and the advance party and
last companies of the 37th had
not yet arrived when the
bombardment commenced. As
casualties from both these regiments
were dealt with and sent direct
to the dressing station.

There was a short but heavy
bombardment of this particular
section of the line.

By the time, at about 11 am, all
the casualties, at this point, had been evacuated
and medical seemed to have
resumed their normal condition, so
I withdrew all but 2 sections
from the front and returned to
the dressing station, where Capt.
JOHN ___ and the remainder of
the personnel had been awaiting.

Except for 21 cases of the 129th
temporarily retained as the
casualties of the morning had
been evacuated from the dressing
station by 12 noon.

Two parties of slightly wounded

were sent on foot to the
trigger rendezvous.

No cases came via the ALBERT Rd
at 4 the afternoon
& all Kahars were withdrawn
from CHOCOLATE CORNER & CAPT
WELLS returned to the two sector,
but 12 Kahars were left on the
ALBERT ROAD collecting post.

On the morning of the 20th the
number of Kahars at the new
collecting station was reduced to
12 under a havil. and SAH. ALI
JAN returned to the evacuny
station.

As there has never been a great
rush of cases and there were
plenty of Kahars available the
Wollisis were not used in the
daylight.

In all cases the feeling of Kahars
was moved began from NOWII
who knew the locality accompanying
those of the other units.

Appendix II for September

Capt. D. Fitzgerald I.M.S. left me in charge of the advanced Dressing Station St Vaast at 4 a.m. on 25th Sept. Wounded started coming in at 7 a.m.
These included

* 129th Baluchis         40
  Connaught Rangers      12
† 89th Punjabis          20
  57th Rifles             6
  4th Londons             3
  H. L. I.                1

* Including 2 British Officers
† 5 cases from this regiment, in addition to being wounded, present Respiratory Symptoms of Gas poisoning to a minor degree, they stated they were gassed by our own gas. Oxygen was administered to 2 of them & recovery was almost instantaneous.
The majority of the Connaught Rangers belonged to a machine gun section & were severely wounded.
The ranks under my charge worked well, and all the wounded except 21 cases of the 129th Baluchis

(who were detained by order of the Divisional General) were evacuated by mid-day.

J.C. John
Lt. IMS.

30th Sept. 1915 —

F. Cob. 1915 /

121/7601

Serial No. 153.

# Confidential

## War Diary

### of

No. 111. Indian Field Ambulance.

FROM 1st October 1915 TO 31st October 1915

# WAR DIARY
## or
## INTELLIGENCE SUMMARY.

Army Form C. 2118.

B1
Vol XIV

| Hour, Date, Place. | Summary of Events and Information. | Remarks and references to Appendices. |
|---|---|---|
| ZELOBES.<br>1-10-15 | The ambulance carried on routine work admitting sick & wounded from FEROZEPORE Brigade. | 1Pm. |
| 2-10-15 | Orders were received at 10 p.m. to close for sick & wounded & march to LAGORGUE at 11 a.m. tomorrow. Capt. REINHOLD was on duty at the Advanced Dressing Station. | 1Pm. |
| 3-10-15 | Closed for sick & wounded. Marched at 11:30 a.m. via PONT RIQUEUL to LAGORGUE (134 1 2.4.) billeting in a school - arrived 1 p.m. The Advanced Dressing Station St Vaast was handed over in the morning to 112 JFA & Capt REINHOLD who returned the unit - all LAGORGUE. There wheeled stretchers and 4 empire & box tent cases were handed over to 112 JFA (stiller with 3 hours of our arriving. | 1Pm. |
| 4-10-15 | The upper room of the school building having been found by 112 JFA to accommodate & care of patients insufficient, they came with | 1Pm. |

Army Form C. 2118.

# WAR DIARY
or
## INTELLIGENCE SUMMARY.

(Erase heading not required.)

Instructions regarding War Diaries and Intelligence Summaries are contained in F. S. Regs., Part II, and the Staff Manual respectively. Title pages will be prepared in manuscript.

132

| Hour, Date, Place. | Summary of Events and Information. | Remarks and references to Appendices. |
|---|---|---|
| LAGORGUE 4-10-15 | Room in their own building | Sm. |
| 5-10-15. | Routine. Weather extremely hot & raining. Cold weather - Miserable jutt until find - | Sm. |
| 6-10-15 | G hislin ambulance will One Sub Ast Surgeon |  |
| 7-10-15 | attend at the dispersal of the OC 112 JFA |  |
| 8-10-15 | for collection of sick daily in dailing. |  |
| 9-10-15 | S.A.S G.K. RANE will leave Armypooras |  |
| 10-10-15 | be deputed to the POPLARS Advances Dressing Station to duty with 112 SF.A. | Sm. |
| 11-10-15 | Routine work. |  |
| 12-10-15 | S.A.S. KARTAR RAM relieved S.A.S G.K. RANE at the POPLARS Advanced Dressing Station. | Sm. |
| 13-10-15 | Routine |  |
| 14-10-15 | One Ambulance stored Kabab in C/o of Salis 23 were transfered from 112 JFA to Scalies 14 were received from the 40 Pathans | Sm. |

Gulab Singh & Sons, Calcutta—No. 22 Army C.,—5-8-14—1,07,000.

Army Form C. 2118.

# WAR DIARY
or
INTELLIGENCE SUMMARY.

(Erase heading not required.)

133

Instructions regarding War Diaries and Intelligence Summaries are contained in F.S. Regs., Part II, and the Staff Manual respectively. Title pages will be prepared in manuscript.

| Hour, Date, Place. | Summary of Events and Information. | Remarks and references to Appendices. |
|---|---|---|
| LA GORGUE | | |
| 14-10-15 | Reconnaissance was founded for those in units were held afoot the reinforcements received. | 15m. |
| 15-10-15 | Routine. Weather damp, cold, foggy. All cases of scabies in hospital were inspected by the A.D.M.S. Lahore Division. | 15m. |
| 16-10-15 | | 15m. |
| 17-10-15 | Routine. | |
| 18-10-15 | | |
| 19-10-15 | The Field Ambulance closed for sick in Indian troops. Transferred to Indian troops. Twenty three cases of scabies were transferred to the 2FA. at 10-30 a.m. the unit marched via LA GORGUE - MERVILLE to ST. 12. 10 a. CAUDESCURE arriving at 12-30 p.m. relieving for sick of the 129th Baluchis | Map Laventre. 36 a |
| CAUDESCURE | 40th Pathans & the working Battalion. | |

# WAR DIARY
## or
## INTELLIGENCE SUMMARY.

(Erase heading not required.)

Army Form C. 2118.

134

| Hour, Date, Place. | Summary of Events and Information. | Remarks and references to Appendices. |
|---|---|---|
| 19-10-15 CAUDESCURE | Sealine Coys & HQrs much delayed in reaching Refield owing to the ambulance blocking their mind on arrival. Accommodation was found in a group of farms, a large barn on one of the farms being used as a ward for battn: Hospital. Fine & cold weather. | |
| 20-10-15 | Routine. Weather fine & cold. | pm. |
| 21-10-15 | Doing R.P. Station procedures on weak ear. | pm. |
| 22-10-15 | Routine - SAS Ram detailed for fatigue duty 112 I.F.A. | pm. |
| 23-10-15 | Routine. | |
| 24-10-15 | Routine. Weather becoming foggy & vague. 1 NCO with 10 colorists from the E. | pm. |
| 25-10-15 | Capt. T.C. John 6th reports to defachet for fatigue duty with 18th Brigade R.F.A. | pm. |

Army Form C. 2118.

# WAR DIARY
or
## INTELLIGENCE SUMMARY.

(Erase heading not required.)

135.

Instructions regarding War Diaries and Intelligence Summaries are contained in F. S. Regs., Part II, and the Staff Manual respectively. Title pages will be prepared in manuscript.

| Hour, Date, Place. | Summary of Events and Information. | Remarks and references to Appendices. |
|---|---|---|
| 26-10-15. CAUDESCURE. | Weather unchanged. All personnel except those on duty went for a route march. Two hours duration at 2.30 p.m. | Sn. |
| 27-10-15. | Routine. Weather very bad. | Sn. |
| 28.10.15. | Routine. | Sn. |
| 29.10.15. | Major H.M.H. MELHUISH. I.M.S. reported his | Sn. |
| 30.10.15. | departure on 7 days leave. | Cpt R |
| 31.10.15. | Routine. Weather very bad. All leave stopped from this date — all officers on leave to return by 7th November. | Capt Reviewer Capt M.S. Off. O.C. No III 9 F.A. |

Gulab Singh & Sons, Calcutta—No. 22 Army C.—5-8-14—1,07,000.

Serial No. 153

44/80
/121

# Confidential

## War Diary

of

No. 111 Indian Field Ambulance.

FROM 1st November 1915 TO 30th November 1915

# WAR DIARY 136

No. III 9th Indian Field Ambulance Vol XV

## INTELLIGENCE SUMMARY.

Army Form C. 2118

C.R. 4/10
6/12/15

| Hour, Date, Place. | Summary of Events and Information. | Remarks and references to Appendices. |
|---|---|---|
| Nov 1st 1915. CAUDESCURE | Routine. Unit warned to be prepared to move early tomorrow by road. Weather very bad - continuous rain and cold wind. | Capt. S.T. |
| Nov 2nd 1915. CAUDESCURE | Routine work continued, health slightly improved. | |
| Nov 3rd 1915. CAUDESCURE | Routine. Capt. J.C. John N.I.M.S. returned to the unit for duty. No. 113 I.S.M. joined for duty | S.T. |
| Nov 4th 1915. CAUDESCURE | Capt. E.H. Reinhold detailed as 9 days leave. Capt. T.E. John I.M.S. detailed in his absence to temporary duty with the 1/1st G.R. 1 Naik and 9 & 6 Sepoys were transferred to R. Mount Brown. | S.T. |
| Nov 5th 1915. | Routine. Reference employment status of O.A.D.O.S. | S.T. |
| Nov 6th 1915. | Routine. All G.S. waggons plus horses & mule transport taken down to the place. | S.T. |

**Army Form C. 2118.**

# WAR DIARY
## or
## INTELLIGENCE SUMMARY.
*(Erase heading not required.)*

Instructions regarding War Diaries and Intelligence Summaries are contained in F.S. Regs., Part II. and the Staff Manual respectively. Title pages will be prepared in manuscript.

| Hour, Date, Place | Summary of Events and Information | Remarks and references to Appendices |
|---|---|---|
| CAUDESCURE. Nov 7/15 | MAJOR MERIWISH I M/S reported his return from one weeks leave to England. Orders received for the unit to move tomorrow to FONTES. All preparations made accordingly. | |
| Nov 8/15 | The Field Ambulance marched at 11 a.m. to MERVILLE, then forming up with the LAHORE DIVISIONAL Column, falling in behind No 7 B.F.A. to march, we continued via ST VENANT - GUARBECQUE - BERGUETTE - to FONTES where place was reached at 6 p.m. just after dark. All personnel marched well, no incidents of culvert occurring. The weather was clear & still but then was favourable. | |

# WAR DIARY
## or
## INTELLIGENCE SUMMARY.
*(Erase heading not required.)*

Army Form C. 2118.

36.

| Hour, Date, Place | Summary of Events and Information | Remarks and references to Appendices |
|---|---|---|
| FORTES November 9th | Routine. Four Gunner Brewers transferred to 193 FA under orders from the Highlands for ambulance before joining Bombay + rifle A.S.C. Convoy joined Divnl. | |
| November 10th | Routine - Capt. FITZGERALD IMS reports for departure on a week's leave. | |
| November 11th | Routine. Weather very less S.13. Capt. ANDERSON reports joins the 5 day leave. + Muleteers from 1 Ainmules with stretchers 1/28 H.S. Regt – 4 mules brought reinforcements OC 1/1st Gunners without leave. | |
| November 12th | Capt. C.H. Rinkels Ims reports takes return from a week's leave. | |

# WAR DIARY or INTELLIGENCE SUMMARY.

*(Erase heading not required.)*

Army Form C. 2118.

137

| Hour, Date, Place | Summary of Events and Information | Remarks and references to Appendices |
|---|---|---|
| FOMES 13-11-15. | All animals rehauled were sent to the Mobile Vet. Section for Mallein testing. S/Sgts Kauler & Seaman were ordered to proceed for temporary duty attached to 113 JFA. | JM. |
| 14-11-15. | The O.B. presented himself for a interview with the O.C. No. 1 of the animals showed any reaction with Mallein. | JM. |
| 15-11-15. | 4½ class shoed on J.B. Barnard reported his arrival for duty. A.B. personnel & horses were Harnessed drill. | JM. |
| 16-11-15. | S/Sgts Teck Chand reported his departure for duty with 113 JFA. Shoeing & B.C. examination of 113 JFA for duty with this unit. Orders are that detachel British horses are being ho-firm reinforcements of "Shutri" being Corp. Depot & a certain no. of Guichars. | JM. |

# WAR DIARY
## or
## INTELLIGENCE SUMMARY.
*(Erase heading not required.)*

Army Form C. 2118.

140

| Hour, Date, Place | Summary of Events and Information | Remarks and references to Appendices |
|---|---|---|
| FONTES 17-11-15 18-11-15 | Routine duties. 11 A.S.C. men + 5 orderlies & their arrival. Miss others received from the MO & the 7 BSC ambulances packed, the 2nd at 9-30 a.m. with the JULLUNDUR Brigade via ROMBLY, QUERNES, WITTERNESSE to BLESSY to LES TOURBIERES arriving at 12-30 p.m. & billeting in a collection of small farms, running close to sick. No untoward incident occurred on the journey, the men were well then & substituted for their vacant billets of hospital (radiant field of hentges) saddle 5 & 9. | fm. FRANCE 36A |
| 19-11-15 | One horse presented with [?] route march at 2-30 p.m. Weather cold + damp. | fm. |
| 20-11-15 | Orders received [?] [?] [?] for a route march at 2-30 p.m. - v my Co. | fm. |

Army Form C. 2118.

# WAR DIARY
## or
## INTELLIGENCE SUMMARY.

(Erase heading not required.)

Instructions regarding War Diaries and Intelligence Summaries are contained in F. S. Regs., Part II. and the Staff Manual respectively. Title pages will be prepared in manuscript.

141.

| Hour, Date, Place | Summary of Events and Information | Remarks and references to Appendices |
|---|---|---|
| LESTOUR PIERS | | |
| 21-11-15. | Routine | JPW |
| 22-11-15. | Routine. To Locality two intersheafs feet. Two were shoals of waterfogon over. | JPW |
| 23-11-15. | Capt. F.T. ANDERSON I.M.S. reported his return from a weeks leave. Routine. | JPW CAREwww |
| 24-11-15. | | |
| 25.11.15. | Major H. MCLEISH reported his departure on leave to England. | J.F. |
| 26.11.15. | Captain C.M. REINHOLD reported his departure on leave to England. | J.F. |
| 27.11.15. | Routine | J.F. |
| 28.11.15. | Captain F.C. JOHN I.M.S. reported his return leave to England. On orders of Res. 5, this Section strikes joined the unit from No 420 Co. ASC lately gone under orders to No 420 Co. | J.F. |

Forms/C. 2118/10

Army Form C. 2118.

# WAR DIARY
## or
## INTELLIGENCE SUMMARY.
(Erase heading not required.)

Instructions regarding War Diaries and Intelligence Summaries are contained in F. S. Regs., Part II. and the Staff Manual respectively. Title pages will be prepared in manuscript.

| Hour, Date, Place | Summary of Events and Information | Remarks and references to Appendices |
|---|---|---|
| 29.11.15. ENGUIN | The unit marched to TILLOLOI at LES TOURBIERES at 12.15 p.m. and marched to ENGUIN where billets were found for the night. Heavy rain for the day. | |
| 30.11.15. BONCOURT. | The unit marched from ENGUIN to TILLOLOI & BONCOURT, leaving ENGUIN at 12 noon. | 87 Fitz Jones Capt. 2nd O/M O.C. 111 Coy. |

CONFIDENTIAL

WAR DIARY

OF

111. Lucknow Field Ambulance

FROM 1/12/15 TO 31/12/15

(VOL. )

Not Transport evacuated on Other vessel.

COMMITTEE FOR THE
4 NOV 1919
MEDICAL HISTORY OF THE WAR

Army Form C. 2118
143

# WAR DIARY
## No 11 2nd or 7th Field Ambulance
## INTELLIGENCE SUMMARY.

Vol XVI

(Erase heading not required.)

| Hour, Date, Place | Summary of Events and Information | Remarks and references to Appendices |
|---|---|---|
| Boncourt. 1.12.15. | Routine. Rain. No guns on duty | SM |
| 2-12-15. | Routine | SM |
| 3-12-15. | Major H. MELHUISH. I.M.S reported on weeks leave to England. | SM. |
| 4-12-15 | Capt C.H. REINHOLD I.M.S reported his return from on weeks leave to England. | SM. |
| 5-12-15. | Routine - O.B.C + all ranks paraded for a route march under Capt J.C. JOHN at 2-30 p.m. weather cold + wet. | SM. |
| 6-12-15 | Capt HITZGERALD reported his departure on leave to England. weather very wet and cold. | SM. |
| 7-12-15 | Capt HYDERSON I.M.S reported his departure on leave to England. | SM. |
| 9-12-15. | Capt Fitzgerald reported his return from leave to England. 11 B. both were clock forwarded to the A.G's office at the Base | SM. |

# WAR DIARY
## or
## INTELLIGENCE SUMMARY.

Army Form C. 2118.

144.

| Hour, Date, Place | Summary of Events and Information | Remarks and references to Appendices |
|---|---|---|
| 9-12-15 BOKCOURT. | Orders were received for the unit, Divisional General's moving Section under orders of the JULLUNDUR & FEROZEPORE Brigades. In the afternoon all Kits were packed and cart-loaded. Capt. FITZGERALD took advance cooking parties to BERGUETTE & LILLERS station where lorries rations were drawn & looked in readiness for the journey. The parties here left at the station when G Lieldon Capt. FITZGERALD returning to Hd. Qrs. In accordance with orders rec'd from the JULLUNDUR & FEROZEPORE Brigades the unit marched as under. Follows. "A" Section under Capt. J.C JOHN- 1M/S at 12 midnight. Proceed to the church north of "A" of "Am" & this there to form the right of "A" in march with total to LILLERS entraining there at 7.51 a.m. "B" Section under Capt. FITZGERALD left 2 A.M. to follows the same route, but the | map HAZEBROUCK 1/10,000 |

Army Form C. 2118.

# WAR DIARY
## or
## INTELLIGENCE SUMMARY.
*(Erase heading not required.)*

145.

Instructions regarding War Diaries and Intelligence Summaries are contained in F.S. Regs., Part II. and the Staff Manual respectively. Title pages will be prepared in manuscript.

| Hour, Date, Place | Summary of Events and Information | Remarks and references to Appendices |
|---|---|---|
| 9-12-15 | 129th BMCHTS - 15 return at LILLERS at 10-51 a.m. "C" section under Major MEIKLEISH at 1 am via FEEIRING to ESTREE BLANCHE there to join the 40th PATHANS, moved to BERGUETTE returning there at 9-21 a.m. "D" section at 3 a.m. following the same route. 15 met the 59th RIFLES (FF) and Sikhs therein at 12-21 at LILLERS. All transport & relieve after entering wills. LESTREE BLANCHE & he under orders of SIRHIND BRIGADE. The Supply Cart with Dr SKELTON returned to-day & also 428 Coy A.S.C.- All twiddle before leaving were settled before marching. | Map. HAZEBROUCK 1/100000 |
| 10-12-15 | All sections returned this morning in this order & manner sealed also with then capture of "A" section who missed the road to some faints & were so delays in | |

Forms/C. 2118/10
(9 29 6)  W 4141—463  100,000  9/14  H W V

# WAR DIARY or INTELLIGENCE SUMMARY

Considered it again further on the march that taking of a cart that they carried to cola at Tilleul's is interim. Arrangements to Quarters with C section travelled with the 45th Pathans. On carneau allowed on the forward section was 3 cows/wagon to the forward each calculated to likely 40 men - + 3 other flats for transport each of which would carry 3 pairs of heads. One two horses found to be ample accommodation in every way. One cows/wagon was occupied by HQ of A.B. transport (henceforth the S.A.S. Division N.O. & the thus the Bearers No difficulty taken was experienced in entraining. The time allowed - 3 hours - were more than sufficient. Sergt WHITTER with "A" section did excellent work in converting the wagons. I should mention with regard to before.

# WAR DIARY or INTELLIGENCE SUMMARY

Army Form C. 2118.

147

## Summary of Events and Information

Here observations that I consider B.C. to D section did very creditably in reaching their halting stations in time & without a hitch. The march was a long one which car about — 15 miles — 9½ hrs — was full dark. There was a violent storm raging. The road was hilly & winding. The Coolies were drawn from freshly hired & downright inferior & mules drivers also new to the unit. The mules (many they without Coverhead) had be delay & hinder proceedings. I think that only extreme care & patience & Coolly Orderly & automacy of the four failed to anticipate

"C" section arrived at the rendezvous ESTRÉE BLANCHE on the stroke of 3 a.m. thereupon they kept hunting our own horse-lines for the HQ Battery with whom they were to complete the march & whose hospital equipment, which they had subsequently to carry

# WAR DIARY
## or
## INTELLIGENCE SUMMARY.

*(Erase heading not required.)*

Army Form C. 2118.

| Hour, Date, Place | Summary of Events and Information | Remarks and references to Appendices |
|---|---|---|
| 11-12-15 | Owing to Capt Engels' [?] indisposition to the Light horse rationing draws [?] in addition before "Gallipoli" & "completed drop" Orders before gun ration was loaded & on the steamer & that train. | Sh/ |
| 12-12-15 | "C" Section under Major MELHUISH arrived at MARSEILLES at 7pm and detraining at once proceeded to embark immediately on the hired ford "ARCADIAN". There being no transport animals available the Cts [?] has he has been ordered from the Quay a distance of about ½ of a mile, they were exceptionally willing but difficulty Capt F.I. ANDERSON I.M.S. rejoined the unit & some cars in MARSEILLES & having come on direct by mail train from BOULOGNE. Serious fever cases were later over from MAJOR KELSALL I.M.S. for the rest of subunit, suffering slight to heavy [?] owing to "Cart" over to the Commander of the "ARCADIAN". | Sh/ |

# WAR DIARY or INTELLIGENCE SUMMARY

Army Form C. 2118.

149.

| Hour, Date, Place | Summary of Events and Information | Remarks and references to Appendices |
|---|---|---|
| MARSEILLES. 13-12-15. | "B" section under Capt. FITZGERALD arrived at the ARCADIAN. "D" section under Capt. REINHOLD and was disembarked also on the following evening at 10 a.m. The kit and equipment of "B" + "D" sections were now handed on board and stowed in the swimming bath during the morning. Kit for tents including to Mangavar, 12 double fly circulars, 9.24 Supt. B's circular were drawn from the Ordnance in place of our marquees tent which were returned. Cabin accommodation was found for the Surgeons and Sub-Surgeons and therefore break space for the G-3 personnel was allotted 15 "C" section on "B" deck "B-D" section being on the "D" deck above. Bell-decks are sufficiently well ventilated and airspace allotted, without being excessive, will serve. Anti typhoid vaccine and anti lymph for use on the voyage were drawn today. | |

Army Form C. 2118.

# WAR DIARY
## or
## INTELLIGENCE SUMMARY.
*(Erase heading not required.)*

150

| Hour, Date, Place | Summary of Events and Information | Remarks and references to Appendices |
|---|---|---|
| MARSEILLES 14-12-15. | Capt Totter I.M.S arrived at 6 a m with "A" section who embarked immediately. All transport wagon vehicles & Stokes ambulances were parked on the quayside and lowered over by the A.M.T.O. to be loaded on some other vessel. The loading party there were loaded on the transport "GEORGIAN". The "ARCADIAN" sailed at midday with the four sections of the Ambulance (Artillery & head-quarters of Ammunition & transport vehicles & drivers.<br>At 5 p.m we anchored at Toulon harbour for the night. | |
| AT SEA<br>15-12-15 | Sailed from Toulon at 8 a.m. | |
| 16-12-15 | Some of the personnel affected by seasick. General health of the troops - Good. Weather Fine | |
| 17-12-15<br>18-12-15 | Uneven passage in the morning. Personnel wounded to ascertain number beginning vaccination | |

Army Form C. 2118.

# WAR DIARY
## or
## INTELLIGENCE SUMMARY.
(Erase heading not required.)

Instructions regarding War Diaries and Intelligence Summaries are contained in F.S. Regs., Part II. and the Staff Manual respectively. Title pages will be prepared in manuscript.

151

| Hour, Date, Place | Summary of Events and Information | Remarks and references to Appendices |
|---|---|---|
| AT SEA. 19-12-15 | Boat personnel exercised on the boat deck for one hour from noon to 1 p.m. Weather perfect. | 1Ph. |
| 20-12-15. | Weather brutal again - of the O.B. personnel were vaccinated | |
| 21-12-15 | Arrived Alexandria 8 a.m. Sailed again at 5 p.m. No one allowed ashore. | |
| 22-12-15 | Arrived PORT SAID afternoon. Orders received for the Ambulance to proceed with the ship to BASRA. | |
| 23-12-15. | Orders received to tranship on to the CITY OF GLASGOW. This was done without difficulty. Health of the unit so far excellent. | |
| 24-12-15 | Left PORT SAID at 6 a.m. Anchored for the night in the Bitter Lake. | |
| 26.12.15 | Arrived SUEZ | |
| 26-12-15 | Report off SUEZ | |
| 27-12-15 | SUEZ waiting for orders. | |

Army Form C. 2118.

# WAR DIARY
## or
## INTELLIGENCE SUMMARY.
(Erase heading not required.)

152.

Instructions regarding War Diaries and Intelligence Summaries are contained in F. S. Regs., Part II. and the Staff Manual respectively. Title pages will be prepared in manuscript.

| Hour, Date, Place. | Summary of Events and Information | Remarks and references to Appendices |
|---|---|---|
| SUEZ - 27-12-15. | Left Suez at noon. | km |
| 31-12-15. | Passed PERIM & ADEN. | m |

S. Mahmud Reyos
Major
Commandg. III JFA

www.ingramcontent.com/pod-product-compliance
Lightning Source LLC
Chambersburg PA
CBHW081359160426
43193CB00013B/2070